Forerunner

Dedication

This forerunner is dedicated to all who have gotten something from it and all who will get something priceless out of the entire book to be experienced.

The gift of these free books (and the other gift of the books for sale) will help make life better for yourself and/or others and it will keep the publishing ministry able to keep things going with work to take care of family by way of your support. Order more books at www.boundtoheaven.org. Any donation will help Bound to Heaven Publishing/Ministries; or simply order a book or two (or more).

My name is Bro. Tracy E. Bush. I am a local minister and author. This booklet is an introduction to one of my latest books titled _A Peace Offering for the Police and the People_.

The Un-silencing of a Killer

The void-noid can be loud like a prejudice person telling everyone or it can be like a silent killer such as carbon monoxide that sneaks up on you and does you in. But if you have your alarm on and it is being monitored by the Lord, you stay protected. Amen and Hallelujah

No more being two-faced against yourself anymore or being snuck up on from within yourself by a part of you that you don't know is there because it only needs to do this one time to cause a lot of damage. You can be a part of making it where it never happens.

The void-noid is a way I describe a newly discovered ailment of a negative state of a spiritual gene that is undernourished and lacking in some of mankind that comes by way of Satan.

There is an air of unrest that is going around the country through the media that has been addressed by ministers throughout the Cleveland area. They are concerned about the possible uprising of people that may be hanging over a case regarding the incident of a young teen that was killed by a police officer.

It is somewhat of a concern of law enforcement, city officials, and other government agencies due to the facts surrounding the incident. I have a different measurement of a good venue of peace that I feel can be brought to the country through my writing and publishing ministry that defuses the trouble that could be.

My goal is to, as soon as possible, get this information contained in this new reference manual for peace between the police and the people promoted as soon as possible in order to give insight to others providing light they may be in need of at the end of a tunnel in order to bring about a new level of grace and love to be shared among all people.

Ministers are putting together places of safe haven for the youth and young adults. To assist with the time that they may be at those places, it is my hope to get them some of my reading material. The thought of the new book can add comfort and wisdom to their lives.

The book offers a possible solution to help prevent violence from taking place but it has so much more to offer that can teach both parties to rebuild truth as a start with an understanding that can help all people know a better kind of respect for self and others.

This book specifically deals with creating guidelines for race relations by helping to make things better and building a new bridge of trust where both parties can meet in the middle to help assure officers that no unnecessary harm comes to another black youth or an officer of the law that gives preventive measures to help improve the entire community. It also helps officers with their ability to become better servants by adding a new level of spiritual wisdom to their resumes to avoid any and all stereotypical attitudes toward others. It also teaches people how to better relate to police officers who are put in place to protect them.

This book is a key to help bring about more peace in this country? It is like a journey to help end a modern day problem, to help with the relations between police and people. It even talks about the fact that Cleveland, Ohio will be the starting place for peace and spread it throughout the country so we all will be on the right track. In addition to body cameras, this could be beneficial as a therapeutic anecdote to help the emotional structure or balance on a personal level when dealing with the element of surprise that some officers are faced with, along with the new reform agreement the city has been order to implement.

It is time to extend a peaceful spirit. This is one of the Lord's blessings that had to be called into existence to be made known to the masses of people in order to help keep peace. This will allow the world to see that changing times have come to this country by way of us getting in line with a peace movement on a new level of thinking and reacting.

If you really want to know of a possible solution to help with some of the problems between the police and the people, invest in a possible solution and you will be better off with what may be priceless knowledge that money can't buy that can help you become more aware. What does the book offer? It offers insight for change with a new bond of trust, brotherhood and much more. It is meant to be experienced and not just read - to knock the edge off of some situations the officers face to help bring about more peace and understanding that is needed between all people, noting that black lives matter, blue lives matter, all lives matter. This wisdom is presenting some of the answers that are needed to help. We can achieve peace on a new level moving forward and moving this mountain of unrest aside as a nation.

What a Break Up to Break Out

What a break up of a way of life that some don't believe or know existed, starting with understanding a process that stops people from growing. The void-noid is like a blackout from people being taken over even though they are awake when they are doing a wrong action. It is like a person who has something bad happen to them and it wasn't good and they can't remember for whatever reason. Now there may be a way for them to stop before they go through it.

Could there be underlying issues that some white police officers have had in a blinding sense or state of being against a person of color, no matter how they feel about them even if they are their spouse that can affect their overall attitude with them as if not being prejudice? Also, is it the same way with black people? If so, the blind spot has been revealed in the book Now to protect yourself get to know what you need out of the book.

If we can save one possible mistake of a police officer harming anyone, we can and should think about adding this heavenly insurance to everyone. If the public knows that the officers of the law are reading this it may help them to read the book, because the book helps people who have a problem in wanting to harm them to stop thinking of harming them.

If this book can save the loss of one American's life, let's try to understand it whether that which is done by someone is innocent or not. Also, if it can save an officer of the law from being harmed by someone, let's try to understand the wisdom to help stop Satan from being the real crook by using someone to do his dirty work.

If this book can save a family from going through the unnecessary pain of losing a loved one to violence, let's try to understand it. If we can prevent the trial of an officer of the law and the pain they will have regardless to what we think, let's try to understand it. If we as a nation of people have a need for more love in our lives let's try to understand it.

If as a Black American with other nationalities making up the whole of me I can say I see a form of innocence in the person who perhaps committed this harmful crime against another citizen, will this hurt injustices of mankind? It is no different with the way I can't judge people. Could there be a deeper answer in the latest things I helped to bring to light? Now can we hold our system to a greater justice that brings about positive change? I think so how about you.

More than enough people have a vindictive way of harming each other and some may do it without knowing they are going to. This happens because of the void-noid sin-drome. Let's change to make a better way of life for all.

Who Needs a Break?

I feel like I am in your presence and if I could laugh I would not. But smile with you even though it has been hard at times. So I can now change with the multitude that welcomes us all. That is a part of my interest that makes me feel like I am welcome. Thank you

For All I Know

It is Worth it to Know it;
It Humbles me to Share it

The innocence I talk about is of a people who are the non-protected not knowing of the will of the Lord that covers people in a spiritual sense that was open to any ungodliness the part I call the void-noid.

To All in the Greater Cleveland Ohio Area

We have to look ahead at the whole picture of what is happening in Cleveland and what could happen the growth of our city is important and if we can head off troubled times from happening.

To the Open Eyes

Learning how to understand that the earthly judge is not totally the real one everyone may want so there decision should not trouble you.

What are the Benefits? Here is One

If the people are dissatisfied over it we can do something about it. In order to stop an uprising of any kind there are some preventive measures that we can put in place. One major one is to give some of the answers to the people who want a judgment to go against an officer of the law and if it comes out to their disliking. They will still have hope that we can carry on without the disruption of an unrest that can make the city look bad to the rest of the country and feel bad about it.

The Time of the Vanishing is over

That is a period that people need to prepare to get free from an unknown force that has a demon spirit of a legion kind that waits to harm them or others by their actions that exists within their spiritual being that has latched onto them in darkness and hopes to come to light with a displacement of negativity in someone's life.

What may cause that split second firing of a weapon may not be a person found completely all the time? A figure on a finger that is on the trigger that belongs to a demon's presence could be the culprit. They can be identified and stopped; point, blank, period!

This could be looked at as a curse but most people refuse to think of themselves as having a curse. Therefore, if we say it is an illness of the mind when someone harms another, people respond to it better but cough it be more than that. Know that if we stop fighting to deny our weaknesses, we become stronger by accepting the truth that creates hope. To know that the cleansing process of the Lord can protect you from the illness of the spirit that can harm people, with one of the best way to go and not by way of the anguish that may come on the mental side of one's state of being that may leave people more confused.

It is like un-voiding your noid to see the foxholes that Satan has placed before you to cause harm to people no matter who. The vanishing of a part in sin called sin nature.

When we all complete working with each other's problems and in ending them we can take our next steps with humility to show true greatness.

Even when I was a babe in Christ, I sometimes got excited during the process of doing wrong and I am still growing. Therefore, I am thankful the new kind of reform as an adult of this life in this time I am within with you.

May the Lord Have Mercy on Such as We

Now before the last trial with the single officer in Cleveland this was a part of what was given. Today with a little more hope in this way that can be a better outlook for others to feel better about because the Lord still has to pass his judgment.

Now if someone has this kind of problem bad enough, it will try to take them over. That is one reason why we need to be aware that the Lord gives us his grace. But if you are on the other side of the laws of the Lord and you have been earthly blinded and if a person's mental state is somewhat crime riddled they are (or may be) really caught up in the void-noid sin-drome that needs a new beat of sound.

Now to whatever level it may be in a person it is there to go against the grain of goodness and it doesn't discriminate, it takes all colors of people, even though there are different categories it like to move or capitalize under. That gives it the best way to start and keep trouble going and growing.

This is a Part of Mankind's Freedom
That they can Have Respect for

If you want to find out what causes the police to do the unnecessary harm to people it may not be what you think totaling it is a part of the void-noid sin-drome.

How to Get a Part of the Iceberg
That Cools Things Off

The void-noid can make some people do wrong and they know it but won't stop like trying to get something free and they should not and if it is with a mob it may even get worse.

Is this also a part of what makes a police somewhat snap in the void-noid and forget what side of the law they are on. Therefore, can we think this maybe one of the best answers we may get, knowing of the void-noid affect and what that is? I am glad we have some kind of answer it is better than none.

The Way Out of a Dilemma

When you are still a part of life one of the biggest things people have a problem with is not getting out of their way to let something get fixed by someone who can fix it. If they didn't create the problem and are a part of the problem, it may even make it more of a problem for them to have to get it fixed, especially if Adam made the problem and only God knows how to fix it or make it go away.

The Message is like growing up
with hiccups that will pass through life with you

Now one of the systems when it kicks in may be their ego in making them think it is right that takes control of them but that isn't an excuse for their actions because hate can be a part of that blinding force to the truth also as was when men burned crosses that defined them with no-respect for the total process of humanity to add to it. Also in some people could it come from job related stress, family life problems or other stuff but, not trying to bust any bubbles I will say it is caused by not enough spirituality, wellness or wholeness that is supplied by the Lord and that's all folks.

Could this be some kind of teaching we need to check out. This is non-political information, it is faith based information. Escaping towerism that makes you think you got power that really isn't good for you.

With This Wisdom

This is one of the things we can do something about to help teach youth this information but to help start a new job marketing plan for work, to help the way the youth feel because if they have no financial stability, they need to work in order to help them make a comeback to the ways we need to start out without lusting for more than an equal share of the country's wealth. This way we don't waste tax money the U.S. Government would spend on this problem. Therefore, we take on the Kennedy attitude of asking not what our country can do for us but what we can do for our country.

To the Officers

Does everyone need to know what's in this forerunner? Maybe not but everyone may know someone who they think might need this. Therefore when you read it recommend it to someone. Tell them it would be better off for you to get one of your own to help the cause. The way you do that is to tell ever one they can at least buy one of what could help so we can get a peace movement started with love.

The book is like a two-edged sword that can cut through on both sides using the power of love to help seal this crack that people are falling into.

Is anyone out there listening? If so hear as many of these words as you can and keep the ones you can use. They create spiritual skills.

The complete book will give you more than enough to help you swallow a spiritual drink made and mix from God's love.

Fundraisers that are fun is like jumping around on a trampoline without knowing where the sides are but feeling the Lord has his net out to catch you if you go over the side.

What Do We Have?

A better way for the police and people to understand the reformation of the officers of American law is being offered. If they do not learn what is in this book you can to try to bring down your defense to walk and talk comfortably to yourself and get the rest you need that will follow. It will be like that and that is the way it is. If I know the situation on both ends there is a middle that we can come to whether someone else knows about it or not.

With this information, you can be your own tribunal with the shepherdship over yourself. Get what can be more than enough of the Lord's love on paper until you work it into your life. It provides a new beginning of spirituality to your life.

This is my way to bring joy to you in an order of first Jesus, others and then you.

It is not a game it is an analogy to stop the effect of the issue. It gives the people a chance to put this problem in checkmate or the situation has been trumped.

This may be a big part of the help that is needed to change the military style which some police have been using.

Time Out

The thing we can learn is like having an officer present with no bullets.

Let's Stop This

We can help stop the aftermath of tragedies before they occur with a new presence of a better spirit that we can share.

We also do this in our country to save face with the world since they look at us as a leader of the free world. We must align the facts of truth and wisdom so all can see how we as a nation can put aside the bad reactions between ourselves and bring about a change that will even out the right process of love we are to be given and to keep the people strong with it without fear to depend upon the system that we have in place to keep policing the cities, towns in all corners of our democracy where all men are created equal even though we have had flaws we are doing the right thing to correct this in ways that can only make our justice system fair for all America.

This will help us keep striving for excellence in liberty and the pursuit of happiness because a happy nation is a prosperous one.

What is needed is a right connection to be understood by the people but also by the police we present to them. It is a non-conventional way we have to go sometimes because acts were not done by a person's intent but the sin nature in them. Only God knows so does he want to punish them if mankind doesn't? From this are we not able to be content? In the past, the job made allowances for a fault to be a part of it. We have not placed (in some ways) fault on the role Satan has in the ways things go wrong regarding law and order.

Now is Not the Time to say
Evidence be Damned; It is Unwise

We are inviting you to join in to end issues. My motto is, if the Lord gives us a way out of a problem, we should be thankful no matter who it came here through. We are looking for your help to complete our mission.

The book has more of God's therapeutic wisdom waiting for you. It is like God sending manna down to Earth from Heaven.

The book is being and has been reviewed by law enforcement officers and is receiving positive feedback regarding its contents.

There may be some who get mad about what I am writing about because they lay in wait for the opportunity to capitalize on the weakness of people who are the "so-called" greedy, by using taxpayers' money like a thief. I am speaking about the fact that we can stop wasting millions of dollars.

My next step is to get out one of the latest books that I completed for the U.S. service people to prevent them from committing suicide.

Now to help close this out, there is another step to help fulfill the needed quota of re-establishing the minority of people who cannot ever be thought of as extinct.

Philippians 4:17
17. Not that I am looking for a gift, but I am looking for what may be credited to your account.

Don't be too cheap to change

For more information, contact Bro. Bush via email at tb.bthpm@gmail.com

Thank you,
Bro. Bush,
A Servant to the World

Dedication, II

This book is dedicated to the future of a better relationship between the police and the citizens with a new kind of blessing and truth.

To all who are familiar with or have read any of my writings before and for those who have not. I can't say I am back because I am here for the first time.

This is a Bridge with People and Police on it
with a New Agreement

This is for the people of the world to know that I brother Tracy E. Bush have fought enough spiritual warfare in the land that people are in to benefit mankind in only the way the Lord wishes it to be. So you can stay out of the spiritual warfare and make not the warfare in your heart your troubles. This is a part of my happiness to share.

Could this be a part of the Lord's therapy? I think so

The wilds of Satan can become a part of the past. If we stop letting it make new history.

Time to stop sitting on pins and needles about this problem

For help: read this book

The information within this book is about spirituality,
not religion!

A way to improve relations between police and people!

If you are fed up, then get in the know. That is why this was written; to create positive change. Some of this writing can be indirectly meant for all who can't read by way of translation not application.

This can save cities the payout for the unnecessary harm that police do which taxpayers should not have to pay.

Bound to Heaven Publishing/Ministries
Copyright 2015
U.S. Library of Congress

A Message With Answers

Let this hit the fan to cool things off!
This is Part of the Big Chill

Could this be the unseen pill to chill
that everyone needs to swallow? I think so.

About this Cause

We don't have to look for the wisdom that surpasses all understanding because it is already here. What is the message?

Who is the Author?

Bro. Bush considers his writing to be his calling that he has been appointed and anointed to do. The greatest high Bro. Bush gets is when he hears about, sees or meets someone who has been blessed by the writing and he said it is only the love of God doing his will through him. Now the new level of writing has given new insight to his life because so many need answers to the way to go in their lives personally and that is what he hopes to offer.

This book contains spiritual and intellectual cleansing properties that can help to save lives on both sides of the fence so no one has to straddle it. with this wisdom, now anyone can inherit the right properties that can help end the curse that time has come to an end and the more who know the less the residual factors will harm others because of all people knowing about this.

You can judge this book by its cover. The book has been developed to settle any unrest between the police and the people or vice-versa, also to bridge any gaps and show all people how to render a new level of truth to share.

What does the book offer? This book offers insight for change with a new bond of trust, brotherhood and much more. It is to be experienced and not just read - to knock the edge off of this situation, dilemma or whatever you want to call it.

The Lord work is not of confusion. The way to defuse this problem is to know that no matter what the verdict given by a judge or jury peace can follow. A new spiritual will through this wisdom is presenting some of the answers to help bring about the peace that is needed between all the people, noting that black lives matter, blue lives matter; all lives matter.

We can be in agreement about the blessings of the big chill that is on in Cleveland, Ohio and also the rest of the USA to get the answer from a book that can help some people from being a crook. The real non-violent presence of spirituality has been released to be known by all. It is time to rewind time to a new presence of a presents of (gifts) over and over again. Now you can cast your cares, concerns and worries on the Lord.

To the other side we can go. We can cross the barriers of all cultures and colors with this new spirit that helps to create a better kind of jurisprudence. It is time to disconnect from the madness, sadness and begin a new kind of gladness. This is a part of the will of the Lords to be known by all. Let us now bind up the nation's wounds to look forward to the 22nd Century.

Within are the answers that are made of and from peace

Foresight

The lack of mankind's understanding combined with prayers has led to answers from above.

What is the Message?

A message with answers for all people about the love of the Lord is ready to bless the land we live in, with the manna that will rain down from heaven, starting with Cleveland, Ohio.

The message contained will bring a presence of one accord as if it is a part of the healing balm of Gilead in the past that we can revisit that will spread all over the USA and maybe throughout the world.

What are the Benefits?

To learn a new level of understanding one's self and how to share love and the enhancement of peace for all people to be experienced by all people during the time of the Pentecost to give it the presence of the Spirit in a way that develops a new kind of love.

News to be Used

There are so many of us together that this is a gathering place of peace. Moving forward and moving mountains aside as a nation.

This wisdom does teach people to child because Satan wants us to keep acting a fool. Don't let him put his two cents in any longer. It is time for some people to learn this is a way to chill until you know what is real.

This ship of hellishness has docked on dry land in a dry dock to not be used ever again to do harm to the people. A new Airship has also docked on earth from heaven. This means an anointing indoctrinating righteousness spiritually holding information positively. We are the new vessel.

We all can thank the Lord for giving us the ability to see a brighter future within a certain part of darkness.

Time to lose the yocky-dock attitudes and mentalities by stopping the free will of ungodly immorally sinning. This is a part of a turning point of a new cornerstone that has been put in place for peace.

Help for the Police in the Country

I, Bro. Tracy E. Bush, would like to extend a warm and hearty welcome to you. It is an act of faith that I write to you in the way of sharing blessings of a higher kind. The one I hope for you more than others is you enjoy these written words. They may enhance the growth within your heart along with the fact that you can sit back and do this in comfort. I will also be adding new words to the spoken languages. I have done this before, but they will be explained. This book does have a different kind of algorithm to its contents but it doesn't have a table of contents.

To help turn around the bad feeling that some people have about the police. We are exposing what could be a or their weakness and informing them also about a problem they can work on to make them a better person and at the same time let the people know that some of the things that they have done that was wrong was out of their realm of control perhaps. Unless they were totally evil and didn't care about the actions that may have taken another life or the pain they cost someone and their loved ones.

There is information to help settle the unrest between the police in our country for the people along with help for the police to be able to feel better on a new process of thinking about how they respond to actions they take when defending the public. This will help stop the unrest and the untruth in Jesus name.

This book has a two way out process of growth. It must be looked at by the officers of the law in one way. Also by the public at large in another way that gives them a presence of not pre-judging someone who has a spiritual illness even though they may have a normal state of mind for the love of all people. Now this may not be a good reason and I did not mean it clears up everything, but it happens and they did not intentionally wanting to commit a criminal act against a civilian.

The information is for the people at large who want answers of why do some use more force to stop or apprehend a suspect. What can I say about this I have never been a police officer but I was a security officer and on more than one occasion had to subdue and restrain those who would cause harm to others.

This is the way I have come up with a part of what may have made a part of 2 the problem a process that goes like this.

A Two Way Street; Both Parties
Walking the Same Way in Love to Make Things Right

To help clear up the racial profiling by police, we can rely on the spirit to do what it does but the people have to do what is needed to help clean up their spirit in the way of fire to fire, fighting in a demonic way of hating on each other.

I personally knew a friend who killed someone during a robbery. He didn't even know if he had bullets in his gun. He went to scare someone out of money being blind from sin. I need not say anymore.

Is this a part of lusting for something someone else may have who wants to impress another by thinking they have control over a life and death matter on a subhuman level that Satan takes joy in the action of welcoming another in his kingdom of hell? Or is it evil that takes over someone? Because we all have good in us.

The trumpets have sounded

All are invited to a feast that has been prepared by the Holy Spirit. There has been a changing of the guard and the Son has requisitioned this and received permission from his father for the changing of the guard to prepare a new way for mankind to see his way out of darkness to add more protection in your life to get you free from a bondage. Now before you partake in this meal for the edification of your spirit, take a moment and give thanks to prepare yourself to receive a blessing in which you may glorify the fact of you still being here and in the presence of the Holy Spirit.

I would say if I were you, thank you Lord for what you have done and what you will do in showing me your love in the body of Christ. Now, as we move forward in our conquest to not only share in the love that has been bestowed upon us, we see a new day of deliverance that is taking place all over the world even in what seems to be the most troubling times in mankind's history. We denounce this illusion of grandeur that Satan puts before our eyes and focus on the supreme being of our father in heaven. We have no reservations to deliberate about these issues any longer. They have been cleared up in order for us to make the pathway to the future and the next generations to follow.

I, as a messenger, announce this as a true declaration of independence from the grip that Satan thought he had upon a generation of troubled people. It is my wish in speaking from the Holy Spirit that no man can ever be an island. Therefore join in the celebration.

On another note, it seems as if at times it was me and the Holy Spirit against the world but that was just a fallacy that I allowed myself to get caught up in and if there is ever anyone else who can say this in thinking it is of honesty, it is not because if you ever find yourself in a black hole where no one is around or no one else can reach you, you are not there alone, the Holy Spirit is there with you. There is one thing some people fail to realize in the darkest hour, they try to put themselves before the Holy Spirit to try to fight a battle. Never again should anyone put themselves first in a battle that they could never win. Therefore rejoice, be happy and in the midst of the battle, stay strong and close your eyes and rely on the spirit of the Lord to bring you out of whatever dark hole you may be in. You can step over, around the void-noid sin-drome at the same time.

There is one point:
The devil is in the detail that can be worked out

We have to look at this as a socialization system to teach people how to change to free them from the self-inflicted negative way of thinking. To do this, we must start with the kids. But now we need to help ourselves as adults first before we can help the next generation of people of all ages to teach them how to get away from this problem.

After all that has been said about this problem, I have titled it The Deaf Ear Death Sin-drome. It is when someone gets caught up in a way of doing something that is right and wrong at the same time by being locked up or lost into a sin-nature that blinds the sight to not allow them to stop a deathly action and just cause a harmful action of wounding someone of inflicting pain to just stop someone. Therefore people in a bad presence of lawfulness or unlawfulness can stop the control that darkness has over them with the healing call a freed ear healing that is provided by the Lord to hear the action that the Holy Spirit gives that is the only advantage you need.

No man may know if they need this or not but if all man knows if it just saves one life ending too soon it is worth it because they may be the next messenger sent by the Lord and that is a price I don't think no one wants to pay. It may cost a hell sentence that hurts beyond any measure that man can calculate.

Meditate on This

People's Contemplation Should Match the Lord's Instruction

Is This A Part of the New World Order?

To the people of the world we all have lost our way in one way or another. May my writing help some find their way home within their heart to clear a way out of a lost part within the mind.

This can help change the people that may be just bad to good on all levels of life. Know no excuses accepted by you.

If I do the work of a Christian sociologist now, could this be that a part of the government's needs that they didn't like at first but may now need? Is this a good moral point of view to be shared? You can renew over and over again. It is to help relieve pain on contact that contributes to the human spirit.

Why do people harm police? Deep down inside they may think they are supposed to take care of their own. The theme of this presence to renew to stop and depart the sea of red blood shed between the police and people is not necessary.

Social ill that is in the subconscious and if they do not fix it they want to kill them. That is not their job. It is to stop people from taking out their social ills on others whether it is harming someone or taking from someone, or they are nuts and that is a social ill also and have a death wish that is a thin line as if they do something to trigger a police to harm them.

Can We Go From Two to Four?

We can change two misplacements of acts that have danger in them protectors of criminals and some of the people who commit crime. But can we also help someone stop wanting to commit a crime that don't want to get caught by having a void-noid sin-drome come upon them and they get caught up in sin of committing a wrong act against someone who harms them and places their own life in a dangerous state of being whether they get caught or not. This way it becomes a 3-way split to learn of the freedom of a sin that blinds people.

Why is the process some good? It protects the people on all levels police people who are committers of crimes people who are the victims of crimes to think on a blink with the Lord's first thought becoming their actions that can save a life or harm. To add even more of a factor to the police health if enough people who may be on an ungodly level of wanting to harm an officer of the law. This gives them a way to see their way out of wanting to harm a public servant that adds a four-way process to help create more change that may add up to love.

Treatment of Today

Will a new way of healthcare micro spiritualism work to change the level of chemicals in the body to fix the bad parts? Is this what the Lord does to repair the goings on in the spirit when it has been tainted or made bad?

Having an eyesight on the inside of self but by the inside of self that can stop an unwanted action that can harm others or someone that is in opposition of what you happen to be doing at a time of dysfunction as happened in the case of when someone doing something wrong and did not have to harm someone but did it for what is or could have been a good person in the world and now he has lost over thirty years of freedom in his life.

There has been a problem with white people and black people being killed by them since they were taken from Africa and brought to the USA before it was the USA. They were cursed with a sin called prejudice and being abused in their nationality by thinking some other people were not as good as them and were somehow subhuman. This sickness still resides in some people. Prayer can help but they may need additional protection of cleansing themselves while on duty at their jobs that can help them understand how to stop a problem of an unknown kind from happening again and have more peace with themselves. That is a big plus to anyone's life. No matter what you do. It is called a conscience. Amen

For the people to help them understand why they may have been caught in a dilemma that got out of control in a way that has or may not have a hidden darkness that needs to be explained so people can see into a kind of darkness that may have fallen upon someone's life that makes people commit an unjust act on someone else that could have been stopped if they were more aware of themselves and their response plus responsibility to what others do to create a reaction that cannot be seen by the inner vision of a principle that cannot be totally explained but can be used by them.

The biggest presence of therapy that can prevent a deadly act from happening unnecessarily is to continually increase the passion for your job. It takes away prejudice in your life. This is something that brings about a stage of joy and gives a stillness of peace within the soul that will allow a sublime level to not do anyone harm.

This book is dedicated to the people who serve and the people who need them!

This information can lead to a better life for all!

Now if you don't know how to give it you don't know how to receive it; that no one needs to be left out of.

The jest of it is to be shared and total up to seeing others as if heaven must be missing an angel!

I have been somewhat of a Kennedy man all my life, especially since I heard him say when I was 5 or 6, "ask not what this country can do for you but ask what you can do for this country." It was exciting but what was my country and what could I do? I had worked to do to find it out but I know work because of hearing it and seeing my dad work every day but was he telling me this or someone else? I don't know. Therefore it is what I do. This one is for you, President Barack Hussein Obama, the president who is not about drama, who I try to fit in with, as if I knew what to do and when to do it .

We Can

Adjust ourselves better when we know things than when we don't.

This book's information is a part of the solution to create more social justice in this lifetime. This is part of what the people should know.

It is time for (if you don't have) a life-saving process in your possessions with you for the people and things are somewhat a man-for-man process where if your man gets harmed and you go out of the way for them, then at least have a spiritual life saving skill to help someone see their spirit on the right pathway of going. Then learn the CPR to stop a place of conclusion for them to meet that may be on the other side for them.

Now what have they had to put up for this problem? If it is a dollar it is not the right thing. But, can we counter the proposal? Yes, but we need help from the police officers. If you get with this wisdom, we can eliminate this problem. At the same time, end the program of the not now need process that people will still have to go through because the ties of the past will steal from the future of the way the money is spent so don't let it become a white elephant that silks the country and makes the budget off side with enough money that you could use to create jobs.

I Do

What two great words: I don't want you to commit to something if the level of negativity is cut in far more than a half by the next 1st of the year 2016 will you add more and let the cause decrease by paying into the sea funding to clean it up. The judgment has the presence in your spirit therefore if we, the people, decide this will you help fix it and could it be two things in one we can help make right with you first then the sea so our shores can become welcoming to the world with peace in mind. Did the USA have a blessing that the Lord now wants to share? You bet!

Take note: then keep up the progress and let's make a big difference in the lives of all people: our new history.

We Can Help Now Stop the Wealth Waste

We can stop looking to the government to help by spending money to do for us something we can do for ourselves. Therefore the money can be used for something else, like to feed people in our country, rebuild roads and the list goes on. Now we can learn to fix the problems of the people and police in the country from what the Lord has given to us.

The Truth

They say this nation is a wonderful thing and I say if we ever get it started right once and for all.

A right connection to be understood by the people but also by the police we present to them. Is it a non-conventional way we have to go sometimes? Yes, because acts were not done by the person's intent, but the sin nature in them. Only God knows so does he want to punish them if mankind can't? From this are we not able to be content? In the past, the job made allowances for a fault to be a part of it. We have not placed (in some ways) fault on the role Satan has in the law and order ways that things go wrong.

The New Social Engagement

To look at people as one people are we in a manner that not only we are equal but we are still an experiment to see if we can become good enough to take the first level of life to the next level? In order to do that, we have to make it through to it.

If we look at one another and treat ourselves and others as spiritual beings living in a human body we all have a better chance to see through our own darkness instead of being mad, sad or unhappy about ourselves somewhat unknowingly in a not so good place with ourselves and it comes out on the other people in the world.

Flipping the Coin

They may have the same issue but in a different way and they get nothing resolve or fix. Therefore, fix yourself first the best you can in order to try to fix someone else even in a way of locking them down because they are in pain. That is why they have trouble. Just like police have pain in life, but at a time of the wrong being done people forget about others and are selfish and want to take out their problem on others. This can stop to not be able to blame others for one's own fault by becoming more spiritually and heavenly minded and earthly blinded to see past the darkness we all must face one day in life.

We Do

Give up a certain level of energy to do what we do. But to not control it as could be is what gets us into trouble. How can this be changed? Give up some of this power we think we have to the Lord and tell him to control the power you may not be able to, to help you not put it in use the wrong way. Tell him and see how he looks out for you.

Hey You

You can become a new you and nobody has to know but you and the Lord. So hip, hip hooray for you.

Stop!

Stop profiling people when you look at them. Think of yourself as someone walking in their step to get through life. Know how to plant your feet on the right pathway; a way to show and share the good will of being a humanitarian. To help create a more unified people, even if they find themselves on the wrong side of the law. You too, must look at a police officer as a spiritual being and not just a somewhat person who wants to stop you from doing the wrong thing because if it was you who needed their help, they would be there for you if they had to, somewhat, whether they like it or not. So think as if we can all get along.

This is a brief introduction off or for a new level of growth to create successful living. This renews the mind plus the subconscious on a spiritual level of growth, in the name of the Lord.

We should know that when the mental has left the station and the spirit isn't right, all that is left is the skeleton and who can work with that.

We can shape the heart that will override all other things we can use to keep people safe. Nothing material can compare with the plan of action that left no stone unturned or it's in there. To lift the burdens that some people are facing in fear without fear does bring a new day to all.

The part of the plan saves lots of money by denouncing the wrong process of growth. The edge that America has found itself slipping into from the beginning of the process has always had flaws to keep us somewhat down. Now is a time to move past the ways we keep moving somewhat downhill, to also giving the dollars where they are needed, that can be put to better use.

The Answer Place

All my people have gathered together and mankind has been listening to mankind long enough; let's change it somewhat so listen to this: the Holy Spirit can even tell you to use your weapons or not.

Do we give up certain rights to be here? I think I can only speak for myself, on a level I have not experienced sense I became a child of God and if I never it is okay with me.

The Pause has Come

If we stop acting like little terrors ourselves, we can help stop others from trying to penetrate our land. Who are the people who are self-combustible who need to move themselves out of the way of themselves and others? I don't know and I hope you are not one.

Gratitude and Trust

Gratitude trust to give your service to others because the past is or has been lived with discontent doesn't mean it will always be like that it can change daily and improve. Become your own teacher. We all have a well in life. Get it out of your subconscious to know your wealth.

Alert to all America

The Untold Truth to Stop the Ghost
To clear up the state of unrest in America

This is a new way to address the conduct of black males in America being harmed by law enforcement officers. This is a part of a spiritual examination and explanation of the cause and cure.

This is a Foresight to a Process that may
Help Clear up Unrighteousness

The facts are an officer of the law has one of the most tension filled jobs on the planet. It has a level of expectation that may be so intense that it takes on a presence of its own at any given time while an officer is on duty.

Therefore in saying this as a spokesman of the Lord's clergy, I submit that it is of great importance that the problems of officers can become somewhat insurmountable in ways that even sometimes the best trained officers can lose their balance and a grip on life in ways that somewhat can't be explained in a sense of pressure that may override the fact of total control over, and common sense from, themselves and creating an inability for them that enables them to have complete control over their judgment.

I say this because they like serving too many exhibit the same kind of reaction when put in somewhat of a precarious position to defend them. It is the dark side of nothingness or a void-noid state of blindness that can come over a person especially when there is an adrenalin rush that takes over their self- awareness that may only see a life and death matter that needs to be controlled and it is up to them to put things under control by them. Therefore, in saying this I will submit to one factor and that is it can become a demonic state of presence that can come into their presence and take over the conscious state of mind that places a person's level of action in an unconscious way of them not being able to control themselves as if they are in some kind of trance of a or in another presence of being within themselves that has dominion over them.

The self-containment of an unconscious act that takes place in someone who is clearly conscious cannot be explained except for a demonic illness has the ability to somewhat take over and control the thinking process that may only get one chance in a lifetime to show up to show out to create pain and harm in a presence that seems wrong for someone to do. At the same time, it will try to be justified by the law enforcement agencies to protect them because of not being able to explain the act on a human basis.

Therefore, it leaves the bewilderment in the people's minds to see an action taken by an officer as a force on injustices that on the other side of the coin looks very uneven and wrong. To bring an understanding to both presence of people, I can only say to keep from inheriting this kind of action that doesn't have the right presence of love with it, we can add the extra power of self-control by giving up some of the control we are supposed to have and understanding a higher creed of growth dealing with the lack of balance of the spirit that can create immunity for us in a free man's state of somewhat of a new presence of being that some may already have but for those that don't.

The addition of blessings from the Lord is a must have presence to get the presence of one's self under control so that an able bodied person can have a better than great chance not to make a mistake that will harm the somewhat or could be innocence in a way that can never be taken back. The pain of this is an enormous burden to have on both levels of the officers and the individual, or families, with the public and even though time will heal the pain, it won't bring back a person if they are lost out of life and we cannot know the love that they may have been bringing to the world anymore. In saying that we can learn from the teaching of what we missed out to teach each other and teach ourselves. I will say you can get under a cloak of adding more protection to the lives of the people you serve to create more prevention and protection for all.

For all of the police officers of the world, you can now be more responsible to the presence you make within yourself by learning a few more things that may add a lifetime to someone else's life by letting the Holy Spirit have a say in the presence of your actions while you are doing your duty. Therefore if we know that the Lord makes no mistakes and he is with us and speaks and he acts for use we can do less (and/or no) harm to another in the line of duty. To aid you and if you would like to learn more, I recommend the following books:

TIME TO STOP LIVING ON THE EDGE. NOW IS THE TIME FOR YOU TO BECOME AND REMAIN BOUND TO HEAVEN? IN LIFE THERE IS SOMETIMES A GREAT DEAL OF PRESSURE THAT CAUSES US TO PUSH OR SHOVE OURSELVES OR ALLOW OTHERS TO DO SO. WE MUST REMEMBER THERE ARE BOUNDARIES THAT WE SHOULD NOT CROSS, EVEN IN OUR DARKEST HOURS. THIS WISDOM HELPS SHOW A WAY TO THE POWER TO NOT ALLOW DARKNESS TO OVERWHELM YOUR LIFE'S LIGHT BECAUSE THERE IS A LIFELINE THAT IS ALWAYS AROUND AND THIS MAY BE THE ONE YOU ARE IN NEED OF.

ALL PEOPLES HANDBOOK. BASED ON THE SPIRITUAL SKILLS ENHANCEMENT PROGRAM. OFFERS A WAY TO RECEIVE ADDITIONAL FAVOR FROM THE LORD TO ADD ANOTHER MEASURE OF BLESSINGS TO YOUR LIFE AND STAY AWAY FROM THE CONSEQUENCES OF HURT, HARM AND DANGER THAT NO ONE NEEDS.

Know that this suggested solution may not be 100% but it is certainly a start. I also feel that the Lord has had put together and in place because of the need for it to show a nation of people how much love he still has for them knowing that they have not been perfect. These two books are not only for police but for all who may be thinking about doing something illegal.

As for me, I can only see myself as a messenger, will you know of this message and help to pass it on so future generations will not feel the wrath of this unknown kind of presence in life that has been exposed in a way like a true enemy in the dark that now can be seen with the need of our eyes being open but from us knowing that it only takes us to open up our hearts to widen our circle of life and our potential to grow without shortchanging ourselves and anyone else. Satan wouldn't wish this but it is also our job to not let his wishes come true.

I have accepted my assignment to give you more insight that may help you with your assignment. Now it is all up to you to do what may be the right thing. My friends and family in the body of Christ I also say hallelujah on our behalf in the presence of the father, son and Holy Spirit.

At Bound to Heaven Publishing/Ministries, we are working with people in more than one area of growth on a complete explanation of this new developing concept of a spiritual kind. Your patience is appreciated because you are not alone.

The complete presence of the process of the outgrowing of the wrong way of placing judgment on not just the black American people, but all people, unfairly can stop by the applying of this new kind of wisdom.

Do some people need a new pair of glazed glasses that have the lens shadowed dark so they can't see their outlook on the way they see things so the Lord can tell you how to fight and win or lose if it be better for all.

To help understand how to help de-root the problem we can look at the past where it may have started in a way of fear. The mistreating of blacks that took place in the past has some deep root that can be cleaned out of the system of some who may still have it. We can put the problems of the 50's and 60's behind us and the uprising of black people that have been harmed by the law enforcement that the blacks had to endure that was unjust, may still have a hold on some of the black people. Therefore, they need to find the inner lock that the Lord can unlock to stop the personal pain so they will be able to look into a new day of forgiveness and put aside the grudges of their inner soul.

How big of a void-noid issue do you have? Do you think or know if you may have one? Does everyone have one? If so, what do people do about it? Are there certain times and or jobs that may bring it up in your life or spring it into action? I think so, the job yes; or the process of being taken out of a routine. It is also that even good people do wrong with the void-noid sin-drome. If a parent of a child makes a mistake of leaving a child in the car and forgetting they are there. It is a way of the void-noid catching someone off guard.

If you think about it, how can this happen? It is from the presence of thought stepping away from the presence of being that separate one from themselves and this is the age old divider and conqueror factors in life as if it presents a division of self. Therefore, we have to protect ourselves and others by being aware of this happening to us, using education and the understanding of love more than we think we can.

Let's say that mother or father loves the child and that is not the issue. The issue is getting lost in a time-zone that blinds them from themselves and turns their focus on the next time zone. They lose a part of their mind or the control they are supposed to have.

So does that make them a little crazy? Yes, but that may be only long enough to do the wrong thing not really meaning it or do some people have an underlying issue with their life and want to change it? do the ungodly except themselves have a control over them that causes them to act sick without them being in control of what they have over this process of actions that can't be answered by me only them and some may not be able to give an answer to that either.

Therefore let's take the fact from the bottom of the hole that the void-noid comes out of the people at a time that can harm them. It is at a time when it can do the most harm. Are we as a people equipped to take on the challenge to stop the ungodly foe by dropping a covering over the place to stop it from lifting its head to separate and disconnect someone from them? I don't think so therefore the Lord has to come in to weigh down the power of darkness.

The void-noid sin-drome is the best tool to kick humans in the back whenever it can so let the Lord get your back before it pops up again like what is still one of my favorite toys, a jack in the box. Let the Lord hold it down for you.

Now there are different skills that way differing but are the same. A person harms by a police a mom or dad leaving a child in a car and it is harmed. But if it has the same result and causes pain it is still somewhat the same. Now how do we justify one from the other? It can't be done unless it is some kind of air of darkness that the person in the act of doing the harm has portrayed or promoted.

The other factor if there is or was a mental deficiency and therefore they were by right not supposed to be in that position of a caregiver or caretaker. The way we can look at them both is do we have the skills to oversee a life and death matter or are we one who will get a bad break in life anyway.

I don't think so first as I said before if we learn enough about the power of love, we don't have to fear these kinds of things happening to us we can become protected. Therefore, we can protect others just by our presence alone because we are never alone.

Next become a watch person for the Lord. If you run into the people who are mentally and or as you may have been spiritually challenged, you can help them the right ways. Get your new skills in order to help others to get there and not harm them on one level or another and knowing they are both there all the time.

There is something I would like to clear up a child's life is precious and we can't determine when the Lord wants to take anyone home, but I have a dilemma. It is my faith that tells all children are returned to heaven. Does the Lord take one of his back in order to protect them from us or to protect us from them and the way they are coming up to prevent them from losing them later to Satan when he knows it he will not be able to get it back. I don't know but the Lord makes you think over and over how I could have lost this level of my mind and thinking. Don't be troubled, God knows what you mean and don't mean.

All I can say is be careful with the most important gift that the Lord gives the in trusting you with his love one being a child that came first and foremost. Now to understand the two way street that goes one way. The void-noid has a way that opens up and it is like a trap where people may do something then they fall in that has darkness in it. The other way is when people are walking in a light and all of a sudden something pops up like a jack in the box. Spiritual skills will teach you to close the lid of the box down. But the strange thing is someone may be winding up another one somewhere.

About me

I had a different kind of relationship with police starting at age 3. I had a bad habit of leaving home to visit friends and staying away too long. If my father could not find me the police helped. This went on for some time. They were a big help to me and my family by helping to find me and bringing me home because I did not know the danger as a child who was out in the world.

What can I say other than when I was a security officer I had encounters that gave me insight like a broke down relationship between law enforcement and some of the people, young black men it seems? Are they somewhat the same in a way of not liking them? If so, one way of fixing up the problem won't do. The youth need to get right in their hearts and minds. The sound of music can help by stopping one kind and replacing it with another. We need to add culture to the lives of young black youth, especially males, to help bring about a new presence of development of a mindset to share in changes in lifestyle, along with a different kind of unity.

No more cop-killer sounds running in the head. Get some back with Bach, Beethoven, etc. then get the books mentioned above. This wisdom in these books will help fix the wrong attitudes and growth patterns of living with no righteousness. Using the understanding for laypeople, the books help motivate positive change in the light of God.

When I was coming up I watched black movies which presented a bad concept of the police officer. Did the movies influence some of this? Yes. By the time I was a teenager, going in and out of the juvenile justice system on more than one occasion, I did not have a negative attitude toward them. After becoming an adult, I knew it was a different world and I saw the light of the Lord when I was locked down. The bottom line was I needed a job. I had an opportunity to be on the other side of the fence. I took it and I became the good then, doing something to help keep people and property safe. This gave me a chance to walk down a two way street so a new road began. Now, in the movies there were lots of bad police officers.

I have been there and have done some of the things I had to do to help others avoid the position I had been in; I knew I needed to help. It gave me a way to talk to the young men and women to help guide them away from trouble and lead them to wisdom. As a security officer I attended training at a policemen's association meeting which gave me a chance at one time in my life and the real had to be revealed and saw the same thing that I was I talk to the youth that look lost when I walk my beat I looked in to the prevent things from taking place and preventing them from doing some wrong and to keep going and keep your nose clean. You can get there where you can be happy and content in life and foremost try the Lord because he has a plan for you.

Now what do I feel was the greatest thing I felt I shared with those who had no self-worth and it required work to build up and they would have to do it themselves also their time and the fact that all people can have a bright future ahead of them and don't be afraid to pay your dues. It may not be easy but you can do it.

There is A Proclamation
(Every officer who joins in gets one)

There a proclamation that I personally feel we as people have to look around for something deeper within. The fact one fact that keeps growing in me about the law officers are in one stage always and that is the more they stop crime the more they stopped sin. The people who are locked up are there to fix there sin in a lot of cases once they are free they can stay away from it again if they find their way out of a darkness that led them to it. Therefore, they may also be one who doesn't know the Lord and they come to Christ Jesus to become redeemed from under their past sins. Therefore the title has a lots more reverence to it name officers of the law. Therefore as a body of people doing their job, how greater body of Christ have they been a part of well I thank God for that because I may be one too.

Do dead ghosts rule in a part of our land?
If so, time to stop them!

Know that the dead ghost of hosts is Satan who wants to captivate you. The living ghost of the Lord is the Holy Ghost!

I Don't Know

People may have to live with more of a wound than the people they have wounded in a way we don't know.

People need to learn about the spiritual wars that go on in their head that can come at the most inopportune but opportune time while people are at odds with someone else to cause them to snap and do something they may not normally do because they have been caught off guard by the negative force within that wants to harm anyone that it can, along with the fact it gets two for the cost of one. This makes both people victims.

This is the plan that Satan has to do his harm to people that hurt family, friends or anyone it can. Don't make yourself available by using the wisdom the Lord gives you to protect yourself from this kind of paganism to know this not a trail of a messianic secret.

Luke 4-18-19
18. "The Spirit of the Lord is upon me, because he has anointed me to preach good news to the poor. He has sent me to proclaim freedom for the prisoners and recovery of sight for the blind, to release the oppressed,
19. to proclaim the year of the Lord's favor."

Some Not

Would say this is a page of pleasantries that show an outline of the content of the material to come in an order. First the presentation of the way it could have happened. A sea of truth that may take some on the ride to find some truth and that is all I know because I don't know what others know unless we can find a way to think alike, so like-minded people who see making it congenial also in the process of sharing an uncompleted issue that can be even more resolved that leads us to a new greater love.

World can you help me see I haven't wasted my love. Please help me see I have not wasted my love. Lord, please don't let me see that I wasted your love.

I let it go to the Lord all of it that made up me the wrong way. I let it go. Now I say it is good to end it, with happiness that the part of you that is owned by the Lord has claimed in you.

I have Waited

There is something that I had to learn the hard way it was there were a lot of things I know but there were a lot of things I didn't need to know.

Time to carry a badge of hope

The Beacon of Light

The light houses not towers are now becoming beacons of light once they get to the upper room where Jesus prayed for his disciples and for all future believers (read John 17).

These are the keys to the service that is to be applied to complete the course of justice in the way to keep all safe and if there is any other measure that needs to take place, the wisdom of friendship and love will be included to keep the peace of mind that keeps the cool head even in the line of fire that can be prevented but if it comes down to it, it will be handled in a manner of love also, even if a death is involved in the action to apprehend or protect the public at large.

Some things will have to be and if so it is to the best of our ability that we include the grace of living in the same process of the grace of someone dying. There is no way around some of the ways people fall but even if the person that you may have to take deadly actions against, will you please if you have learned anything from this including the last right as a human to ask them if they know the Lord and tell them if not will you accept him as their Lord and Savior and you are sorry that this happened and if they say yes, you will see them in heaven.

The biggest concern in some cases they look for a confusion of the crime but gets the confusion of the way they will go that is beyond the world we live in. Don't wait on any man, do this with the blessings of the Lord on your side because he will be by your side if you think like this and act like this. This is the greatest of therapies in the world.

I try to not do much thinking on my own without prayer. But when I do I may come up with something good and I believe it is the greatest time to share love with the ones who help to keep the law and order. Therefore, it is my wish that all people share in these moments of a new area of peace between us.

I Know We Are Ready

To know now to travel through the tunnels and caves that have been shot down in the lives of people because of the darkness that brings fear on someone life. Therefore inside of the brain we can learn to travel through the dark side and not let it trap or shut down the pathway to freedom.

The neuro-transmitters that once closed in on us or close us out can now run freely in order to not be placed in darkness. I think we can be ready to pass through the caves in our mind and they won't cave in on us to trap us where we won't know what to do next to keep people safe around us and or not be able to see in the darkness because we now have night vision that requires no eye glasses because it is an inner sense of a perception that only can be given to someone who studied and is approved by the Lord to enhance their growth beyond what any man can teach or be taught by any earthly prisoner of a curse because the Lord only can grant this wisdom to you that surpasses mankind's ability.

The ending if the beginning gives you the lift that takes you high enough to make the presence known that you have no power over life and death but you are a mediator to the one way of a safety faction that must be put in place in a sometimes uncivilized state of confusion that you have a goal to only bring to a resolve to do your best to not harm anyone unless it is no other way with regrets about it before you do anything that may make someone shed a tear. This is the truth with the Lord as your witness at the time of your judgment day.

It Isn't Your Fault

When someone else loses their joy and don't care about anyone else.

Breaking News

At Bound to Heaven Publishing/Ministries, we have developed a proposition that we feel can create a declaration between the police and the people who are outrageously disappointed and apprehensive over their actions to bring a solution to create a new attitude and a peacemaking presence of state between all parties.

We do this to save face in our country with the world but to align the facts of truth and wisdom so all can see how we as a nation can put aside the bad reactions and bring about a change that will equal out the right process of love we are to be given and keep the people strong without fear to depend upon the system that we have in place to keep policing the cities, towns in all corners of our democracy where all men are created equal even though we have had flaws we are doing the right thing to correct this in ways that can only make our justice system fair for all America.

This is a change of guard in some people from the inside out to keep striving for excellence in liberty and the pursuit of happiness is because a happy nation is a prosperous one.

We are inviting you to join in to end the issue. My motto is, if the Lord gives us a way out of a problem, we should be thankful no matter who it came here through. Selah

All Honorees

Some can say is this a kind of faith healing process of humanitarian appreciation of life to really help once you know you have understood the cure it will help to cure many, stopping towerism today, if they have some level of this!

Now, if the republicans/democrats can get some growth within themselves, it can trickle down to all parties. Who need control when all can agree who trust is it that needs rebuilding, if not ours with the world in one or more ways.

We Can Tell Ourselves

We can't get a better level of wisdom, knowledge and power then what we will learn to not become, a part of the endless place in darkness. In my life right now, today, I am thankful for this pathway to a new kind of light that reigns sincere in my heart.

I now can't accept any kind of unknown challenges that come from darkness that will put me out of the light of the Lord now and forever.

On a Lighter Note

Some would consider my writing a continent of consequences that develop a group of worldwide best thinkers.

Fulfilling a need of people can somewhat break you in your pocket I have been there and done that and ended that kind of living because I found a new way to help.

This process of offering this kind of treatment may be on a pioneering stage. It beats a blank, don't you think.

This is a new delivery of a modern day present that has been around since the fall of the tower of babel. This includes a diagnosis also remedy for an ungodly spiritual unseen sickness of darkness that can be explained. This is a part of the unseen enemy.

Now we all may have a little towerism in us but it hit's the multitude on a godly level because we all should want to go to heaven and with God we are protected and its foolish to get beyond that by not seeing yourself as a child of the Most High.

The process of this can be looked at in a light that when the people in towers came to a level back in the day they went hunting and almost or could have, if it didn't stop, kill off all Rhinos and they act like a buffalo, who they almost killed off also.

Now don't get the lazy-ism to stop the problem, it is to a sickness need I say more. A potential cure is available to help stop the towerism mentality.

The lower level of towerism is Rhino-ism, which is spreading out, not going up, of anyone who has the towerism went through the rhino-ism that attacks people of an echelon of politics and business like an element such as carbon-monoxide.

Keeping it True

If the people are not ready for a change the government will not be either so people are ready for a new kind of change that is here.

Forgiveness

The process of this word works in many ways one is to forgive the people, places and things that may have harmed you. Next yourself in a way that can only come from you being human. Then me for not being able to give you all you may need but all you need to start if I left out anything that could help so help me to believe you will think of and put in place the rest of the right information you do need.

Thank you
Bro. Bush

God's Spiritual Therapy (hereafter referred to as "GST")

We are Only Human

The ordinary facts of being born that come to all that bring the trials of confusion can be a part of growth. We stop growing in our wealth when we become eluded from the second phase of growth that applies the learning process of wisdom to all of our actions. It is a fact you may not be able to receive your human rights until you receive your spiritual rights: God's first, mankind next.

To stop as much of the harm to the people in the world let's take the wars in the Middle East as an example. First we can and must accept the first part of it as a spiritual war that has become a ground war with in use.

Therefore the production of the right way to ease the casualties that take place in war people must have the right guidance from the Lord. Next if there is a better way to resolve a problem of whatever level. People need to look at which way the Lord gives to you to not win but stop the wars.

There has to be a mediator who was chosen by the Lord that he has chosen to give the people a way to create a positive change that doesn't make more war but peace between the people. This process has the best results to be shared by all people.

To be used to tell about a way or more to get and keep in order to stop falling into the upside down lifestyle

Does towerism only affect the people in high places? Know that it hits others who are in a position that gives them an authority over others. The number one person that may get caught up in the issues are law enforcement who may find themselves lost for a period of time on a level that puts them in a position that they become over taken by the use of the power in a job and one of the worse could be a police officer.

The spiritual disconnect of a rational action doesn't compute in a way that they are overtaken by an unconscious process of a negative action and it can be seen that this has happened for years especially with the white police officer and even today. You can find this in the news all over the country because just being connected it might not be the right spirit to be hook up too there are bad one also to get protected from.

Now the thin line comes with the hate that some have in being prejudice but for some we can't add that too. It is just being overtaken by the blindness that Satan places before them to act outside of their own control.

What can be called or should be known as the same or better and latest sports craze, needs to rise up out of the ashes. That should be love by more of the people that the love of sports to make a happier American get with the sport of learning all about them. It is spiritual skills.

It is no game. It is real see for yourself once you have learned about the process of growth you can receive along with the good you can do. Now bless your own heart. The Lord allowed this to happen it makes him happy.

GST

What are some of the symptoms? Not being able to control or in control of the action that could have resulted in the prevention of taking a life? This may only happen once in a lifetime to someone in that position but all it takes is, once Satan only wants some people on one level to show up for him and do his will and once that happens, it can and may create enough hell in a way it has not a chance to happen or there is no need because of the damage it does to people's lives along with the fact the police officer that leaves them in most cases trying to justify an action that Satan has used them to commit against some as if they are the criminal in the street but may want to harm and kill someone.

The wolf pack posse mentality b.k.a. void noid has had its place within the police departments in this country and it too was a group of officers who were under the spell of towerism. This can also happen when almost any group of people gather together.

Now don't get it wrong there are some good people who can out of the muck and mire of the past that are the builders of the great lighthouse and are not affected by towerism. I would not want to offend anyone and the job they do. I only use them as examples.

Towerism is the destroyer of a process of growth that got handicapped or crippled by Satan in the spiritual gene pool of people all over the world. What it does is increase the opportunity for Satan to make his move in someone's life to harm others in a way that can't be seen by them to a certain degree and sometimes it makes them where they don't care one way or another, as was in the 50's and 60's in the South.

The tragic part of this is when there are people who care about what they do and say and get caught up in the sickness that Satan causes by their action of not being in control of something they think they are in control. The two for one hit and Satan loves that more than anything: it is called straddling the fence.

Get Them Freed From Sin

The biggest problem that I think we all need to be aware of is the power of towerism by the use of a weapon, a gun. It is a sad thing to think of a piece of metal that can help to create death. Satan has a bond with some people that once they put a weapon in their hand he waits until he can come in to use them to do the wrong thing before they know it, and if they have an issue or two it makes it better for Satan to distract them and cause them to do his will.

News:

A Place to Stop (to be Black) in a Sense of Loss

This problem adds to so many other problems like a kind of bola-bola. It is a part of the problem that pushes blacks over the edge with already dealing with their somewhat inherited issue of having the opportunity to have available a gun that makes them feel like the tower of power is on their side and it is their enemy when we give some real thought to it. It also affects all nationality of people because it makes them feel bigger than life as a person that is a curse all by itself In that minute they thought they have the power over life and death, which is one of the biggest curses on the planet earth. Just this alone, that not one person has the right to have.

GST

The truth that is life behind all I do to bring a new level of understanding to the people of the world is one big thing the goodness of the people outweighs the bad. We can increase the goodness in people who are still lost within the blindness of a level of what can or has been planted in some people by the principles of Satan because it is so real and it is a fact no one will get harmed on his intentional level of losing their self-control if we are protected by the Lord plus knowing Satan's dead and all that remains are the principles of the dead spirit that he possesses of its self.

To Gain Light

See the Darkness Disappear

So if we know how he works to make his principles come alive in us and know it takes the Lord and us to stop them. We can keep ourselves in the daylight of our blessings without the interference of the Prince of Darkness taking a life that doesn't belong to him because he never gave birth to anyone. He had not one child and he tried to make believe he is some kind of father of a part of the world and what some people make the mistake of doing is believing in him without knowing and one of the first ways is to not believe in the Lord then thinking they know the Lord. These are the most useful tools he has that harm the people of the world. Therefore get in the know now. Who is really on first and that is not you.

Napoleon said something that define reality and give hope. He was a great man and a conqueror but the tower he was in did not have the Lord in it with him to teach him to know when to hold the cards he had and know when to fold them. That is the Lord's job to teach us that but if we can't hear him we can lose everything as he, and other leaders, did. He fell from grace regardless to his achievements now personally I think it is better on earth than to try to regroup in hell. Food for thought I hope it doesn't give you a bad taste in your mouth.

Warning
GST

Satan wakes up the killer cells inside of the dark part of the spirit of people that everyone has but the Lord keeps it in control to not do something that is wicked or evil that leaves death and destruction in the pathway of life for the most ungodly ways in people who are unprotected. Please do get over this sickness it can be done.

Tip, Tip, Tip
To keep moving up

If you are not learning to hear with your brain and not with your eyes, find the part of you that is the closest to your heart and work on it, work with it and let it lead you when you think the Lord is not around and this will keep him around and then he won't take his hand off of you to let you find your way because he never really takes his heart off of you. Know no matter what you think.

What could be one of my biggest pleasures? Reconciling lives before they die. Chalk this up to color and help to not only see with your eyes.

As a police officer has to make a decision in a split second, which is when the Lord can make it for you. That is what spiritual skills do for you. The gift of spiritual skills gives you a way to become the scrip analyst to breaking the code to a way out of Satan's grip. We can defeat the known and unknown enemy in this to see a way to the therapy of it all.

Now with skills you don't get left in a position that you did the right thing and it is but it looks and feels wrong because it could have been prevented with another split second action not to do something that may not have to be.

Train up the Wrong Way

They take a good reason and create a bad occurrence of gain materially. I am referring to a group of people who are too weak to fight off the demons' parasites that want to destroy them. What do I do with it? The way to avoid it is to dismiss the "it".

Who are the Blind?

The injustices only come by way of a people being blind to the truth of mankind's sight to be able to see the truth but more so to be able to admit to their wrong they do to others and if a sickness of darkness is in them, it hurts the truth in them maybe so much they hide from it could this be some kind of peek-a-boo time to get scared back to the truth.

There are people around the world who are being hurt by the radical and this program of helping change the wrong way of thinking can help stop some of this also (especially since we are making things right at home).

May you continue to escape the curse of the darkness that has been placed upon mankind just because we are mankind.

An Addiction

Is something that stops the connection to the higher power whether it is drugs, sex, eating or being lost at a time they should not be, etc.

Big News

The skills that the Lord gives you provide the power to take the scowl of your soul that only you can. That may be the one thing that can create unhappiness and you won't see it coming, as the youth who was killed, that hurts the police officer who did it.

This is a part of the melting heart project that puts people on one accord with a new generation of a loving presence.

GST

This is a big part of the misguidedness of people that people are visually numb who walk into darkness. It is like seeing the wrong and still walking into it; the unfortunate.

There is a spiritual darkness out upon the world that needs to come to light. Could this work that I am doing be a part of it? I think so.

Beware (of wrong thoughts)

Think on it
GST

We are so much alike when Satan gets a hold to us no matter what we do, when the wolf pack mentality gets a hold to us, we go under his spell for example. The police officers in Cleveland, Ohio and the people of Ferguson, Missouri lost control the same way in a sense. This was the same way it may have happened in heaven when Satan persuaded the other angels to create a gang to try to take over heaven by fighting other angels. If Satan has or had the power to convince angels to turn against the Lord, who do we think we are as humans not to get caught up or off guard?

We have to win. That is why we must get under the Lord covering to protect us from ourselves. It is real; the only place to find the safe haven we need, Thank God for his protection.

GST

The Lord is not a Lord of confusion. He is the Lord of organization. So welcome to thinking on the right level of thought.

May Your Signs Increase
GST

Like a red tail hawk because they have 5 times the sight as a human but may you lose the other traits they have if you have them, to mob up on others or intrude on other species that comes near their home even if they are innocent, like a gang mentality that makes them lose their bird mind.

To Further Add to This Process
M-N

Now everything that works for good works in genesis to stop the ways some people will go through revelations without getting harmed from something they do to themselves.

Togetherness

Is this a way for you to say yea and I say yea so everybody can say yea simple pleasure. I turn you on now you turn someone else on and on.

Not If

If a black person is killed in a span of time in the USA, then why not at least cut it. Also let cut the first to last with a new kind of membership the love that starts off a new lead or repetition of decrease on any suicide levels in the world.

I have learned the birth place of my home gives me my roots of the start of my life and it all ends up where we come from. To home of the spirit and not just the brave because I learned to be brave in a purpose of the Lord. Can I pass this along to others to help make their lives better.

Reformation
Time to Become AN S-S (Super Sport)

There is no excuse to do the foolish things that people do now that you know about.

It is not by the will of man that this will succeed, but by the will of God that wants to create change in mankind. Therefore once they receive the message the misunderstanding of the wrong principles will turn off and around. The test factors are in the results that can't be expressed on paper. The final figures are compiled by the Lord.

Now
GST

When we take it whatever it is we're going through we are able to make it to whom we are supposed to be in the first place going through the battle fields of life gives us the guts to keep it real so spirit up. Don't look down or break down.

It is Nice to be Out of Zero Land

I once had a sickness of a spiritual kind it somewhat hurt me in more ways than one it was the shame of me once I took a good look at me and it I wish that people that were prejudice would stay that way because they go to hell. It was wrong to feel that way and I felt like I knew it but, for whatever reason, I was not able to stop it immediately. I felt because of what I had heard and had seen at times in my life it was okay to feel that about what they were doing to hurt others.

Then I changed. It happened in a doctor's office when I was watching a friend's son, who was about 5. Another child about his age started to play with him and the parent said "don't play with him, they are the devil. I immediately said "no you are the devil and you should be ashamed of yourself." They left and I was not ashamed anymore and I knew I had to stop thinking it is ok for people to be prejudice because they go to hell but the little child did not deserve that so I prayed that parent would get pricked by the Lord to change for the child's sake. I did not care until I let the Lord work on me because he won't until you let him.

To The World
GST

Too many people are trying to save face and they think they are looking different to the Lord. Why? The lack of being in touch with a reality that counts for nothing more than a self-glory trip of I see me better than you see me and I am what matters not you. Oh well, what kind of blindness do we really have in the way of darkness that some people create a light in that makes them think others can or can't see into? Is it the light birth unrighteous side which is Satan's darkness that some people get trapped in that one day will end their light?

Help Stop Prejudice; Get Skills

The person's way out of the ungodly hate of one people of another skin color to another people of skin color. People must believe that beauty only can be found under the skin. And if no one knows that they are blind to the truth of life and are lacking love for their own lives.

When you interact with helping people make decisions, please explain what is troubling you and what you think may be your best exercise of therapy to give you the most for your effort because we want you to not waste your time and energy. Keep an information sheet every 30 days for 3 or 4 months. Look over what you wrote then do it again, rewrite the essay in 100 words list that the first time that should be 300 words at first you will give yourself a self-examination and you grade it; don't just make yourself look good to you on paper, but feel good about your life. The Lord is helping you write the evaluation on what you feel is changing in you for a better way to like you and what you do. Besides, your progress can't be judged by mankind for the learning about you with the Lord.

If you like you and don't like what you are doing, change it. You can find your way to a happy job that will give others happiness also in your life and out of your life because that is one of the best things about life.

This may seem like a tumultuous way to apply an anecdote that can revitalize dead bones, but try it anyway and see how you feel. When you complete this book, start writing.

We can learn to let the right spiritual state of being reigned over the carnal state of being. This is one thing to keep up front in your mindset as you write out the ways out of the wrong side of thoughts and turn it into the right side of thinking.

Two-Fold, I
GST

The project of teaching police to detect the spirit of mankind with the power that comes from a higher space and place and time to get an internal note of love that allows them to see farther than the skin color of a person before they act on a human level of process the help they need can come to them with the wisdom to apply what is right in the different situations they face daily on all levels of being a servant of the people for the people. This job may be one of the hardest jobs that have to be done, to equip them with every advantage that we have, needs to be put in place.

Two-Fold, II
GST

On the other hand, we must teach the young people of color that they must learn to put themselves in the right state of mind by way of their heart that may be in need of some kind of repair because it has been broken in ways of not only disrespecting themselves but the respecting of others therefore the repair work has to also come from the higher power of the Lord that will result in the new attitude of love for self and others and knowing a friend and not being led by whom they want to be a friend to keep them on the right track.

Attitude That Can Help

I see the misplacement of the young state of mind and it needs to be put back in the right level of the process of growth. I feel that if they had more of the Lord's intervention that could help save them when they get to a certain level of growth when they are responsible for themselves.

GST

There are lots of people who are talking about cameras to see what is going on in the process of police and that is good but to add more from the other side is to equip the people with a new level of thinking that gives them the insight to not put themselves in the wrong position in the first place.

GST

The Lord is foreseeing the problem before they show up in the lives of his people and gives us a way out of them but sometimes they have to be hit by them before they act to create change but his answer to the problem is always there and the prayers have been answered all we have to do is open up our hearts to receive it and if the heart has become hardened then it makes it harder to get into. So open up your heart and don't let hate close your life down from not being able to grow past it because we sometimes may not get another chance to do the right thing. Do you feel me and it doesn't matter if you see me just know what is good for you in your heart.

The Greatest Gift One May Get
GST

As a human we can receive is to not take our fights that we may get in when we are some place we don't belong in the first place out on someone else. We all go through some kind of spiritual warfare and we may not even know when we are in this kind of fight and due to our being human and get into it with someone else we may wind up taking it out on someone because we are blind to the darkness that Satan has put us in.

Therefore we somewhat know we can't win with in this kind of darkness but we can win with on the human level with someone else. Therefore we wind up harming someone just to think we are going to be a winner that makes us a loser of the fight with Satan by taking another person's life.

It is the tale of two tales that kills humans and leaves the winner the biggest lose because it may cost you your eternal life and you can't see the right for being wrong after the damage is done. Stop and read the message that is coming from your heart and not your mindset.

How much reading between the lines do we need to do?
It's up to you

Now who gets hurt in lots of cases more than others in this way are the children during the time of break up. It gives Satan a perfect excuse to put some people in the blind to catch them off guard because they are lost out of love and feel they can't live without it and at the same time don't want love to live within their other half without them.

The powerless that makes Satan make them think they are powerful in a sick way of harming but with the skills the Lord has waiting for you, if you are even one who has this come up in your life can get through it and come out right whether you were right or wrong in the relationship.

The number two level of Satan getting people to do his will inside of the warfare he tries to create is the gang fight he is an expert in this because he lost the first war and now he takes advantage of the offspring of the Lord because he lost the first fight so his principles have made him successful in winning with this level of fighting that can start over a pin dropping in the wrong way.

So if you think what you may be doing in a fight don't think too much for yourself, let the spirit in you take over and the heart back you out of the fight with a two edged sword that can cut more than once. Blessed are the peacemakers!

Who are the Blind?
GST

The injustices only come by way of a people being blind to the truth of mankind's sight to be able to see the truth but more so to be able to admit to their ways they do to others and if a sickness of darkness is in them it hurts the truth.

Super Sport

Is a good sport equal being spiritually skilled. Or is it the best one of the best things people can always keep telling themselves "I am not smarter than myself that has a part of the Lord planted in one. It will help to keep you humble to cope, heal and move forward.

Police Officers
GST

The police can de-escalate the actions not to escalate.

This is part of the Lord's spiritual declaration that is better than the presentation.

People act better on camera but people are better when the Lord is guiding them.

Some of what I write about is only a process for peace my fellow brother bush

The wolf-pack mentality even had the pedestrians join in without the police being indicted.

The botched presence of a non-growth of life leads to not having spiritual skills. We can start by learning to stop it. It is best to heed to the Holy Spirit.

This is a non-traditional way to help fix the problem
I Hope Not
GST

When you tell the truth they call it propaganda. What can we do about it? Keep telling the truth that is all. It will work in time.

To the Children

The best thing we can teach the children is to police themselves and they do that better when they see us police ourselves. We can help take the nation out of turmoil please.

Skills to help you be who you are supposed to be

Attention Please
For the People

To all of you if you were a part of the marches demonstrations, rallies that took place across America, I thank you for the adrenalin boost I got to forge ahead with the work I feel I have been called to do and complete this part of it to help bring about a peaceful change in what is a flaw in the American system in the law enforcement process of treatment that now there are answers for even though I must say it has to be repaired on a spiritual level I hope you can give it a chance again. Thank you

Get a better line of defense, at Bound to Heaven Publishing/Ministries, we are offering them the process of getting started of their safety program to keep more people safe including themselves at a time of what could be an arrest taking place.

It is the intention to put no one in danger on both sides of the process. That is why an inner sense of balance will be placed on the conscious and subconscious to activate integrity of the spiritual will that can add foresight to the process where it superseded the process of what may take place on both levels to protect the law officers also in the process of the action to safely arrest someone if needed.

Goals to Have For All

Our aim is not to decrease the law enforcement officers' ways of protecting themselves out in the field but to make things more officer friendly to the public and increase their truths that the public has when they see you and have an interaction.

You may say it is an inner peace that has been somewhat taken away from some police officers that have a missing link to a heartfelt process of growth that has to be replaced or repaired, one or the other it may be as simple as that. What to do about it? Add love and pray. This will be a big step in completing the repairs to fix it and finish it in the will of the Father.

We fight for liberty for the world in the USA. Now did we bite off more than we should have and kind of slipped on our butts? If so, not any more, whether it be a choke hold or a gun to harm a citizen of the USA by a kind of fluke.

What is happening?

I am basking in the glory of the Lord; knowing you can't put a blessing from the love for and from the Lord in a book. It got out some more from what you have read.

The Unfolding of a truth help to stop
the right ghost at your doorstep

Are You Afraid of the Truth?

Spiritual skills provide a new way to help repair the spiritual house in you to give you a new attitude.

Stop the Uphill Climb

Time to make things in life stop rolling downhill on the people and look at them roll across the hill.

The Lord Gives Us

The right ways to disconnect us from the way that haunts us from the past that has attach us to ways such as racial profiling prejudices and as an example; it was my grandfather told me when I was a young child I was a white boy. He kept this in my mindset and it made not think of the race of others in life. It helped me grow without prejudices and it was by the will of the Lord I never let the race card hurt me; it worked. That was an eye opener for me but it is the Lord that had him do this to give me a way out of this kind of darkness that others had that was around me. Also, to see the spirit of people without a darkness that could have hurt me and stopped me from doing what I needed to do in and for the world.

On Point

Police can start policing themselves and let the Lord help.

In Order to Not Separate

The church from state, I would like you to take the words spiritual skills inside of the book and every time you think you can change it also to moral skills. Do it now and look at it as I added good moral skills a development of a new level of humanitarian character. Therefore, within this process is the ability to not have the illness of racial profiling and more of darkness.

The process of learning to not feel or feed into the process of an ungodly presence of a state of mind can be overcome with the ability of nurturing more love for your fellow man but some find it hard to love someone outside of their own race of people because they don't want others to feel equal to them. That is a blinding phase of life people don't need to live by.

Don't Reject

When anyone is at the lowest point in life, the Lord will come along and place upon you a set of angel's wings to lift you up out of any kind of misery.

My sympathies to all the families who have experienced harm of a loved one on any level whether non police or police in NY, NY or any city.

Let's stop this kind of grim reaper in our lifetimes.

People Can
GST

Police the police. New laws to protect the people may be special prosecutors can be put in place.

What do I do?

What I do is help teach people how to believe and understand what they can't see or hear that has a development of damnation on and in their lives that is beyond a secular level of the abnormal that comes to steal, kill and destroy the human because it is a spiritual fight that blinds anyone who doesn't have enough faith and belief that they are not equipped without the God given skills of the additional blessings that are needed to know what kind of fight their in with the Prince of Darkness that they can't win at all.

People Need to Stop the Bad Part of Protesting

We must see the opening in the armor of the country we live in that at a time needed a new concept of growth. Now here is what the blessings of the Lord has done for us to stop the powder keg placement of people as it was before thank to the foresight that we have now.

Today may the Holy Spirit stop at your home. We can learn to have the right kind of constitution of spiritual health to gain a spiritual intuition. Hear this word. Will all of this work completely only the Lord will know.

Satan has been putting this measure of defeating and defrauding the people since his exile from heaven to blind the people and he places this in people's lives without them knowing and being aware of what he is doing to make a molehill into a mountain. He has used the ploys on the common man as well as on kings and keeps it in place with the thinking of tyrants all over the world.

That is why he needs to be exposed in order to bring more order to the world to know to look to the heavens for your strength and not to yourself because you can't withstand some of the kinds of storms that Satan can put you in along with the fact if you think you can it is then a no win situation for you and all involved.

Therefore, let it not be your fight that you are fighting at a time of day or night in at dark places that you can't reach in a physical sense because it does nothing but make people strike out to do harm in an earthly sense to harm someone.

I like the song I am a loser and I don't like the way it appears to be how about you therefore change it. Don't let the melancholy about the new placement of a mindset that leaves the playing field so the Lord can step in to do what he can do without you getting in the way as was before others trying to do a job they were never meant to do. Now do most people care about what is right and wrong? It is not for me to judge but it will be judged by God if you do not want to learn the ways of God.

The place of peace to share with all people nothing bad ever happened there. It is a part of the Lord's house we can go to on earth to honor him that is special.

The Best Therapy in the World

How nice to be sitting in an upper room it is like sitting on top of the world without a need for a dime in my pocket at this time of life. Knowing no amount of wealth can compare to one of the best feelings anyone could ever have is the might to try to make it right in the ways that can't be seen by anyone on this planet but the Lord in his glory at its finest now you may have to get out of the presence of thought that is a sea of green to see the blue sky that is without the smog of the world keep in mind that ignorance is blind, change that.

It is enough to be blinded by reality but to be doubly blinded by Satan it is not okay. What is the shame of it all? It is a damn shame that some people don't get a chance to learn of all ages so let's change that.

Truth

Being spiritually stable may be in a way better for some than being totally mentally stable so in order to get on both pages become leery to know your true weakness is not a show stopper to believe in what can be done with the power of the Lord in your life.

R U 1?
Police
GST

Do you believe in an eye for an eye? If you do, then you are living in the past. You need to understand how to turn the other cheek in reference to this statement, whenever you are called out or have to pursue someone who may or may not have committed a crime you should know that you will first be on a level of putting a warrant out for them in your conscious state of mind. Next you will want them to see if there is a further process that needs to be taken. Then once you come upon them, you will need to warn them and if that doesn't do your next step should be to wound them. Do not become a smoking gun, one who smells sulfur before it is released into the atmosphere.

What ever happened to turn the other cheek? Stop the western gun fighting state of mind. There is a myth that has always been projected where there is going to be a gun fight in the media in reference to a television show. The show has a good moral balance to it but when it is first presented, there is always a fight between someone in the public and the law. Therefore let's eliminate the start of anything with a "Gunsmoke" level of thinking. The next level of thinking relies on another television show that causes a similar affect when you are out and have to go on the pursuit of a possible wanted criminal. What we want to do is change the status on that from "Wanted Dead or Alive" to just wanted.

There is a certain level of tower power that comes along with a job as a law enforcement officer and what has to change is the factor of this to a light house. Then, deflate self to being a servant to the people, even if someone may be in a position to harm you. Now it may seem a little nutty, but you have to think like you have to protect them from hurting themselves from hurting you.

The Need Had to Arrive Before You

All of these points of reference were put together before you needed them. The Lord has this done to come forth out of darkness and until people got tired of the same old thing, it wasn't time to bring it forward. Now it did take time to get here but it started when this country was born the second time by way of another nation of people coming here and starting of policing it in a way that wasn't right. But that is history and now we move forth to new days, though we can't for the past and how many nations of people suffered great pain to bring this day to pass also were the protectors did not do the best they could because some didn't know how.

The people of color have suffered enough. Therefore, if we are to stand as one nation we are to think like a melting pot of all colors on one accord.

What may be one of your biggest tools in life? The fact is it is never too late; point, blank, period.

Topside

One of the hardest things for me was to always keep in mind I was a part of the Lord and he loves me. The way to the upper room with the Lord comes with knowing this foremost, this is a way to get you there. To find out more on this read John 15-17.

We can learn to have the right kind of constitution of spiritual health.

To gain a spiritual intuition, hear this word.

The new model is for all police to also have spiritual skills under their breath; to protect the people that they serve. This model goes beyond race, it is a journey for the self-justice that could save a lifetime headache for an officer of the law to not jeopardize his eternal wellbeing also because mankind can't really judge your actions but the Lord can when it is protected by the law for you to do what you do to serve the people.

I don't mean to be afraid anymore but it is offered to give you a line of defense that you may not want to cross because mankind can't help you.

Don't let your job cost you a hell sentence

I Implore You

Now can this be most of the light that we need to see in a pathway to a healthier America.

To go by a Bizarre Principle

Can this be a way to stop the uprising of the people that Satan wants to set up the USA to bring the dead who serve in all branches of the armed forces to a state of turning over in their grave? Well if so let's stop now.

Not Just One

Rebuilding the infrastructure on the inside of people and the country is a two-fold win-win process of achievement. Now let it be known too many cooks can foil the meal that has been prepared by the Lord he may only use one as was David's on the battlefield so enjoy the fruit of the spirit that we all can share in too end this kind of hunger made from love .insert I feel the hunger of your belly

One Man, One Plan

If the Lord has stepped in to help fix some problems we as humans are having can we accept it? That is the question you have to answer for yourself or do we ignore this? Please say no we are not going to turn our backs on this plan that has been given to mankind by way of one of his messengers.

Now if the Lord gives it to me to give to the people, will you use it that is my question? I hope and pray you will to help stop the violence in America we can keep it simple and remember the Lord is orderly.

Now is this a way to revere Paul's word or to create a right kind of revelation with?

Am I an activist? Yes, but I am also a deactivator. Also am I a leader? No a follower of the things I have seen in my lifetime to get behind to learn how to do something about. Why is this? It gives me a greater sense of purpose to follow the way people have been given to learn what they need so I can put my needs behind me. I don't try to fight I just go with it.

A Foot Soldier for the Lord

I have been writing for over 40 years and have over 30 books completed and never had an outside publisher. I did the publishing myself with no major success and gave most of them away to people who needed them. Maybe it has been that way because I am a spiritual writer that feels the Lord does my writing for me and it is really his words I use to put in an order that I hope makes people feel better in life. Therefore I will think in line that this writing will not fall on deaf ears and will create peace in the USA.

The work I do in the body of Christ may be a soul shaker that brings about the fear in some that makes them think it may rain down fire on them but don't fear the Lord will be with you to become a your shield of covering if you are in his covenant.

Americans

If you want a new way to create peace and not just a new day, the time for it is not near but here. Time to freeze frame this process of growing out of a dilemma as we have done in the past and as others have done that created violence to make it known that the people are really looking for a peaceful means to stop an issue with the "powers that be." At the same time to not reenact the things that we are doing while going down the same old bitter pathway of the way we get things done to get the right results, if the people are now ready to stop the unlawful way of the police.

We are accommodating peace at this time of year so it is the Lord's will to add his special job to it that is what I believe.

Stop Now

The pound of cure that is offered helps to stop a larger chain reaction in and on a worldly level. If we are not in line with what we claim is the will of the Lord by way of our charity that we share with the world, in also the area of leadership, along with the fact of what we display to the world from our process and madness, we could lose some of our allies, we have built up over the years, in ways that we are not able to see that weakens our defense in parts of the world that may come back to bite us in the back by them turning their backs on us. Therefore, look deep into your heart to see the truth about all I am writing to you about together one again on one accord as if it is a time for jubilee or even the sanctuary of the Pentecost is upon the land of which we have fought for the loss so many lives to keep it free.

Now it seems like the people in the land are threatening to harm themselves more so than anyone else could ever. We have a blessing on this melting pot we have so let's keep it by way of the one fact that gave us a new way and that is how much we forgive ourselves plus try to fix things to stop the harm that might come to our land in the USA.

Now Are These some of the Facts

That makes the missing element detach or not be seen that stops a thought in time of there is no black hole or void-noid in our pathway on this level of earth that we all live on. I thank God I don't need to go there the way we save the distance we have to go to, to collect ourselves has been shortened. Our concentration should be on the salvation of mankind to see our heavenly creation produce a lamb in our care and the warmth of the son upon their care in our land.

A New Rule is Necessary

We don't have to or need to be in a positive that makes us look or act like we may have another psychotic episode that tears down our business, vehicles and people get harmed and locked up that cost more taxpayers and the people who get in the mess that may result in time locked up or money that can be used more wisely.

How ridiculous it is to have enough money to burn a wet elephant with and don't know what to do with it. It is dumber than dumb.

Thank God for May

May the spirit of peace fill your hearts on a nonviolent way of showing the expectations that stopped in America, on more than one level. First, police repairing their system within to end in a not likable future about the way they feel about theirs also.

To stop and prevent this kind of fever from continually spreading, look at the aftermath of anger unhealthiness divorces abuse in family drinking, drugging the feeling bad because of the loss of the love ones in their life. The need to know how to move forth with love may be hard but it must be done with the Lord's help.

This we can help prevent because it is like falling from one level of darkness to another as was done when the man who was with in the void-noid state and try to kill his ex-lady friend and because he had no control and had a problem with the problems the people and the police are having he kill two police as a satanic act were he had so much darkness in his way of growth he black out as Satan wanted him to do.

GST

The following scriptures are suggested for reading: Psalm 91; Psalm 112; Psalm 115; and Psalm 138.

Sometimes I have told myself I don't know much but I know that I know enough now about love and the lack of it.

A Need to Fulfill or Not Fill

I have dealt with people with the Jim Crowe attitude but I will say it is kind of ugly but People can feel a change on the inside once they admit it is wrong because no one need to be in that rank and add to their detriment it is not worth it, don't you think?

The Eliminated Measure That is in Place Now

It is not a skin problem but a sin problem. The unknown now are some black people that live in the darkness of all colors are truly the law enforcement agency in court and out of court does black people make more white people sin I do not know. I would like to de-process the process with a way to try to help make things right.

One of the problems that some people have with being a good super sport is they don't want to grow up. There are also two divisions about people: they may have a good heart but their head is somewhat upside down or their heart is upside down and their head is good. Oh well get well now it can happen; bless yourself.

People can stop being in a state of dissolution with themselves and not trying to place it on someone else. Then when they can't get some stage of disappointment at them with an unreal madness appears.

We all should stop letting the right things filled up with wisdom fall on deaf ears starting with ours first. We must clear up the harming of the people who protect the communities of the USA, it hurts me every time one is hurt trying to do a job that can call for a sacrifice of their life. Those that are fellow comrades have an inner sense of revenge but must never forget that vengeance is the Lord's but being human it still can effect some on an unconscious level that had to be prayed out of them, themselves.

An Understanding of Why Therapy is Necessary
GST

Now if you have some kind of idiosyncrasy in you that may be undetectable to you, it too can dissipate or disappear within your process of growing subconscious way provided by the Lord that he may be aware of that the Prince of Darkness has attached to you the Lord will remove.

Minimize

There is always some kind of taboo that is linked to a job like a police officer, which may require taking a life. It is a mistake on it that has the reservation of harming an innocent person not intentionally but unnecessary. Therefore in saying this, if there is any kind of tool that decreases the chance of this happening, I hope you as an officer of law enforcement will get trained in a way to help decrease this from ever happening.

It is the same on a different level of judging and prosecuting someone. The facts are in: too many people are being locked up who are innocent. You too can find a way to come into a laymen fellowship.

To Help Stop the Problem
GST

What kind of towerism do police and law enforcement officers have to deal with personally that takes them off the mark of loving the people they serve? All we need is love to help us as humans to serve first to make it easier to see what I am talking about on paper, love requires food/nutrition to live without it there is no love because people would starve to death. Next protect love how with more love. Now if we don't protect love what do we get death in one way or the other fast or slow.

Therefore if we don't have the right understanding of how to protect love, we have failed to get fed the right food of how to or knowledge and as we live we are sometimes confused about how to love a spouse. Therefore, if we meet with what could be seen as an enemy, how do we treat them with love in a life and death matter?

A new and right way to address the conduct
of black men in America by police officers

It is time to clean up and stop the untruthfulness and unrighteousness of the wrong kind of treatment of men (and women) from the law enforcement in America. We do this with an explanation of the cause and cure.

It breaks my heart to think a youth got killed in a toy store or playground. Did the shooter have the void-noid sin-drome that pulled them into a black hole of darkness before they knew it? All they could see was to put someone else in a black hole, no matter where they are or the age they may be. Is this a self-preservation action that could be made as challenges in truthfulness in a higher court of the Lord? Do we make it known that it is because we need to be skilled by the Lord more so now than ever by the Lord again? Why would they kill so fast? I think it is their fear of or from their soul with it telling their spirit it is going to hell. Therefore it has something to lose and it is a somewhat unconscious reaction that may be controlled by a demon spirit that is upon someone. It does not have to be a police. It could be someone who tries to rob someone and at the time they did not plan to harm anyone, it just happened. Therefore we don't play with fire power because we see what happens when a child gets hands on a gun and I think that if you are not a child of the lord you may not need your hands on one either along with spiritual skills.

An outline of the new way of understanding

Well, there may never be the right way to approach this dimension of action because it takes on sometimes a character of disbelief in a way that it is hoping the outcome is something to be proud of, at other times it doesn't. Therefore, is the love we try to claim perfect not so at a time and do we know enough about it to work with all the people at home the jury is still out.

Now what about the foreign countries? Well that is up in the air also. So now we look at self and how genuine is the power we have to understand love. I will say to you I am one who is still learning to love himself and if my writing is an extension of my love for me I have gotten a long way to go because if what I write doesn't affect my love for others, it is far from the mark I thought I am supposed to be at or am I there.

In saying this, don't let the problem that someone else has become an eye for an eye, turn the other cheek. Then it is a good chance they will learn from their mistakes and also grow in love. Now may be the best time to learn what is written to grow love in your heart. Now who is the enemy or bad guy; someone who did something or someone who did not? Don't be so fired up to jump on someone who know less about love than you do, especially if you are not trying to teach them something they need to know, because that may be who you have less love in your heart than you want to believe it is; think about it.

If I am the voice that is crying out to the people who need to be heard and the Lord has chosen me to be the spokesman and if it is okay with people to do this talking up as a forerunner but just for them then it is wrong because if I am to show a new way of love I must also show it to the other side of the coin also because love doesn't shortchange the one who may have a strong hold on the one or people who are doing or trying to do what is right but have an unnatural way of actions because of the lack of love in the lack of love in them and they wind up doing something wrong not meaning to and I can't say that is the case but if it was a mistake and an honest one, it is time to heal and forgive because if I turned my back on them, it is along the lines of letting someone die alone and it should not be that way when there is hope to mend a broken heart and here is so much needed needles and thread to be used. The Lord has sent to his people use it, it will last forever. It never wears out.

Now this can also help people stop some of the violence in the country to show them something they can learn from this. We may be able to help their spirit to lift them out of a street life.

Now it is man's writing even if this gift from the Lord is not by the people. They can't say the Lord has stopped making a way to show them how to build more truths to give more love in ways that can't be counted.

As a Nation

We the people must stop the energetic-irony energy that is running through our veins that makes our senses numb or null and void that keeps us till and stuck on stale that steals from us by us not moving forward in a way that shows the love we have for our God in our lives. Replacing it with the still waters that run deep down in our soul to where there is peace in a new way to know justice for all mankind.

Last Comes First

The process of injustices have not just shown up on our doorstep, it has been in place since the new breed of people came here to do the right thing but did the wrong thing at the same time. Therefore, it is believed by me I think and others it has totally ran its course on all levels in all arenas. Now can we get moving along to fix it? Yes, if we see the truth about our nation as a people.

If the last straw has come out of the haystack with the police issues, then let's be the first generation to claim victory over the ending of a system that was wrong but is now being made right. Now we are marching forward in the right manifestation.

Do we now use this level of thinking to move forward or do we let the ungodliness that we have come through keep us from uniting as a people can't at the same time looking back and blaming the "founders" or forerunners process of a kind of injustice that handicaps us as children who can't outgrow a way of pointing our fingers at someone else all of the time. We can't figure out what is wrong instead of going back to the drawing board and figuring it out. If we read something once and didn't want to understand it just because that is the way we may have felt regardless to what was written one way or the other.

Or

We are just going to run from the truth until we all fall out over something that we were born to start out to find our way out of the darkness that we were put here to do before we all can see the light. Therefore, let's not make ourselves tired in the pursuit of a happy life for all people. We are not a cursed people, we are a blessed people who are able to clear up the messes that come with the territory we live in and stand by.

We the people of the USA are not trying to create a revolution but a reincarnation in the spirit of the people in the Holy Land that is felt from even mountain sides and from sea to all seas to see a new light house in each other.

It is the wishes of the Lord that his words make people think, act and rejoice to know how deep his love flows through you and upon the land we live in it gives me great pleasure to revitalize the purposes for our lives as he wishes with us and for us.

To Me; For Us

There is one thing that as being human that troubles me. How long must I stay alone in the wilderness running from civilization before I am out of the woods because it won't let me in, a black man with other nationalities in me as well as a big bright heart to share? If the Lord says it is time I am rejoicing. Will you join in to end a war we have been fighting in darkness that is now a part of the light?

We Do

Stir the soul with new spiritual moments

Know This Place in History

There is a fact that there are people who have always been a part of the black struggles that are of all colors. Now more so than ever one of the reasons why they have felt the discomfort of what it may be like in a sense because of the perpetrators who have been dressing up like officers of the law and the negative placement of them harming all folks but more than less it is Caucasian. It is like it is two blind spots that made one because it is not right one way or the other.

Will This be Seen?

This factor creates a fear that can be known by all people. What an outlandish part of a down side to help all people see up. Ps and just about all the time it is a Caucasian that is doing wrong. If not we as a people have to get others to follow also if we stop harming each other senselessly then others may become the same. Therefore get suited up.

Get in a New Covenant

To the Police

It is time to stop going out on the battlefield unclothed daily you need to not just have a bullet proof vest and cameras, you need a spiritual covering of a shield of God's presence of peace and love to know if you fall you will rise again and not a presence of defeating all that you come in contact with.

Therefore, the use of time is on your side and on the other side of who could be the unrighteous lead to do the wrong thing to not mistake one from another for the sake of their salvation.

People should not condemn those who come to them like an alien because he doesn't look like you want him to. The one some past over that brought the news of the coming.

Now what we do is help fix the policing but the people who need policing. How we am in need of us all working together to help stop the crooks because all may not stop unfortunately but if we have more jobs it will help to put the money into jobs for people help stop crimes of all kinds.

The hope can be put in place to have a safe city with a police department that is accountable; where justice can be served the right way.

Big News

We can have the new kind of representatives of the present of justice in the USA in our police presence in the name of the Lord.

Today the people are on a great migration to jubilation in change as the people left Egypt to go to the Promised Land but if we can't all hear the Lord it will stop short of the place the Lord wants it to be. Therefore, hear these words and welcome to a new kind of promise land just around the corner just past the shack.

This is a contemporary phase to create a new atmosphere in the spiritual space in peoples' lives to increase a better human level with the horizon to stop the past tense of not being right in our lifetime with a better temperature to cool down the atmosphere.

This therapy has the wisdom to give an escape clause from going into the void-noid level of darkness.

Sometimes the hardest part of my writing is it is a love affair and now to let go is like I hope you have one also. The beginning…

Eat hearty my friends, this is a meal that can last forever

People can stop running so fast they run themselves inside out and expose themselves to a place where they cover themselves in fear. Fear not my friends your underdog is here.

The Date Has Been Set

The facts are in: do you understand that you are a witness? The trial started before you read this book. We have cross-examined the details. It led up to one imposter that has perpetrated the crime through the blindness of the people. Therefore, we find the defendant guilty of being a human but the real master mind behind the plot is Satan. He uses the unwise and foolish to do what he can't do. If you are not ready to be blamed for something that someone else does from the power you have been given by the Lord as a birthright, then know what and who you are dealing with in order to not become a pawn in the ways of darkness.

Fooling around with fire power will get you burned and it was told to me by my mother, who I think was some kind of angel, to lighten the load of blindness as a joke. She told me she didn't want to get cremated because she didn't want to burn twice. It took me a while to be able to laugh at that but I now understand she wasn't going to do something wrong. The moral of the story is don't you do anything outside of God's laws to get you burned working with Satan and do it to mankind because it might get you burned in light of the justice system and also wind up with a hell sentence. Therefore, get free from the double sin. You may find help in a book I wrote, *Freedom From Satan's Zone*, which could save you a jail or hell sentence.

Knowing the fact that no one should have to be a slave forever in the presence of self that two mindsets are set up in to do the other harm must be stopped by you at first to become first as all people should be now and forever. To see forever you have to be forever instilled with love. You have love so use it right or it can get lost from you and then you may wind up on a trail that gets you burned.

Now, who needs Satan to plead their case for them in front of the Lord saying that he earned their soul and the Lord loses a child of his to an eternal hell sentence. What kind of justice is that or what kind of armor do you put on in the morning before you awake to protect you from the wicked one that is lurking about inside of some of mankind who wants you to do harm to others as well as yourself?

How can the blind judge the blind when Satan has committed two sins. People are really the innocent ones who get caught up in with a darkness that shows up to do all people harm? We can stop it if we try.

It is hard to convince someone when they were used by someone who could not be seen at the time and at the same time, we are a people who like to do harm to ourselves and don't know why because we won't listen to what we need to protect ourselves and it is a fact that people will make you pay for the injustices you do that you can avoid by learning to stay away from any place or thing that has a connection with the void-noid sin-drome that wants to steal your peace, joy, happiness and life.

Now no one has the right to do wrong even if the earthly law say so and we as humans don't get away with anything so if mankind gets it wrong, don't worry, the Lord doesn't. Therefore, don't create more destruction for anything that opens the door to the void-noid to come in at a protest rally because he will come in and stab you in the back.

The void-noid also can make some people virtually numb and if you are stagnate and it is like a kind of being dumb not aware of what may be going on around you. This places you in a position of not being equipped to fight or defend yourself. Therefore get out of that position. You are like a standing duck that is ripe for the picking or getting tarred and feathered. That is not pretty and that is what happens on the inside of you. Now who needs to feel like that? It can only be felt by you and not seen by others.

Not I Said the Wise People

Now this is not an excuse it is a wake-up call for those who think they are grown, but are not in a way of being protected as a child of God and doesn't know what it means and how to think and act.

The footprint that we leave should be made from growth and love if we are a part of a group that is like they were in the 60's that was peaceful like MLK taught. It is a good thing but if there is one bad apple, the group should put them out as if they were or are policing their actions so lots of people can't get into a rage kind of riot that gets people hurt.

GST

Now back in the days the people were beat down, kicked down and dogged down. They wanted peace and freedom. They say that there were spies planted in the crowds to start trouble so beware of the ungodliness that wants to harm the innocent. This should be done by the police to police themselves and remove those from the police force to keep things safe.

GST

We can't let ourselves become divided or some will try to make us fall and we can't afford to allow Satan to slip through the cracks against us. It causes too much harm to people and it can weaken our economy as was with the cost of the towers that fell. What kind of good we should have done with that money.

We the People

Know now that we can dam up the ungodly levies that have broken up the flow of fear between the people and police because the one fact that the fear is a tool of Satan he has put in place that harms people that set people in a rage to harm others sometimes before they can stop themselves because of fear. Therefore, we denounce the fear in our lives that can harm someone. This is a possible way out of darkness to defeat Satan. We will have no fear in the name of the Lord.

Don't Just

Shop with the cop, feel the spiritual connection with him and you too.

Could this Work
A Cop Said

Cops can't cure society's ills, it is a path to foolishness and the people think that we are lost to finding the real answers that are right before our eyes and ears without using our heart.

Now could it be that when someone gets killed by a police officer the inspirit of love in someone get mad or sad because they know that the person that got killed didn't have the Lord in their life and feel bad because they didn't share this with them so guilt drives them to cause more trouble.

I had a problem with a man once and when his life ended in a violent way, the spirit of the man did what he did when he was alive somewhat went through his mother's house slamming doors and cabinets. That created unrest in the house and after his mother moved out, the next people that moved in had the same problem and they left and the house had to be torn down. This was a wicked spirit.

When someone gets killed by the police because of a wrong act, they may not have had a right spiritual light because they felt they have something to do with being a hell raiser that affected their thinking of people that are not out of darkness themselves. Well I hope not because all spirits don't leave the earth as are supposed to because of being trapped in darkness and can't go into the light that may influence some people the wrong way on an ungodly level or way.

What can be said about this or is this an excuse to do the wrong thing by some that without being right destroyed and stolen property and cause jails to be filled up all because a bad spirit of evil that has nowhere to go but around and around? Does anyone really know? I can't say because it is the same when a good spirit leaves the earth sometimes but in another way that may cause people to act the same way somewhat to want a new change.

To Live Blue

To live blue means being a part of the blue wave that is going around the USA.

Do we need spiritual skills to help us get the spiritual bad teeth out or our mouth to help us not just think but say the right thing? Also know no pain no gain.

Do the Super Sport
Towers

From you, you get the power to step down when it is time? I think so do you? Now it is like the tow is in the house of God at times.

Now is this information one of the Lord's latest ways he has given to us to wash not wish the gray away for us to see sin before we commit to it whether it is to lie, steal or kill?

This is a part of God's therapy or therapeutic nutritional insurance that all people can use but the officers of the law more so because of their duties. None of mankind's abilities can take anything away from a chance to stop it from adding more blessings to life.

I have taken the time to put this together; now will you take time to understand it and use it?

Help Stop Prejudice (all kinds)

It may look like prejudice but it may not be. It is only a tool that Satan put in place to make people look at others with a somewhat hatred that creates pain because someone got trick to look at the bad with in themselves. Then the negative feed off each other which produces harm with misunderstanding on two levels because someone got caught off guard show up by Satan using them to commit sin. You need to know we can stop him from laughing at us.

Explanation

Saving cost equals life to the people.

A Possible Down Side That One Must Face Alone

Now if a police officer gets caught off into a double jeopardy trap doing the job that the people not like the way they have done it, then they may catch a ticket (for punishment) from the Lord for doing something ungodly, but or even if we can't see their heart to know if it is right or wrong.

Now for anyone who wants to act like judge and executioner you don't get the sentence so don't do it for God's sake to save yourself. Now I am not saying all of what I say is correct but it makes you think and if you find something wrong in the book it belongs to me.

The Catch 22

Does towerism power harm become a part of this and or could this be a factor?

Hebrews 7:18-19
18. The former regulation is set aside because it was weak and useless
19. for the law made nothing perfect, and a better hope is introduced, by which we draw near to God.

This information may just be like a release valve for the nation to let go the pressure and tension and pain plus fear that it is carrying because of these issues.

This way to persuade or go is an unconventional counter measure of reacting positively about how not to become that requires no terror and pain of anguish that comes after the wrong reaction whether it can fall on you or someone else's physical presence can stop in this clear guideline that comes from this spiritual development.

This may be one of the only things some may need or want to add to their life along with the fact of what you may have learned in one or more of the books I have written.

To anyone who has a sickness of a private kind: get help or keep it to yourself and the Lord.

The new iron curtain that will be let down on the demons of darkness to keep them out is available to everyone.

The Unfortunate

We can shake down from the tree thinking a Jim Crowe status of darkness that some may participate in that has an unseen problem on this level and don't know it.

When Doing the Peace March

Know not to ever poke the hornets' nest in all groups or rallies; to the people of any kind of gathering.

Who

We even got to look out for phonies playing police. This is the real sick mind that is sin driven and has added to the fear of the people I think they need help and to be locked up for a long time, not just a slap on the wrist.

At Bound to Heaven Publishing/Ministries we are helping to turn a public perception that we need an answer for use to help us understand the right kind of principles for an answer to the problem. It is you who have to make that final or find another answer.

To be able to have the sense of presence to help stop an act of the wrong kind that can happen to people in the country, we have to do something different. The best part of this process is the Lord controls this so civilians of all kinds and all other people even those in government can grow into a state of pause, which means preventing abuse using self-esteem, to move forward out of themselves first to see the sea of people who have trusted you to not trust yourself as a present that cannot even be touched by anyone that it included because you may think self-consciously that you are him in more than one way that blinds you to you first, then others. When it is to be the other way around, you put people first and no lobbyist can pay or play you off.

Does Satan do all he can do to tear us apart and down? He does; so why would not he play two ends against one another if it works? It has worked for so long why not keep using it? Besides he traps more white people in it to do harm to black people. Then anyone else since it used to be the original people of Indians that they did wrong for so long until it too had run its course as will also the black people.

Know that prejudice didn't come from mankind. It came from Satan who planted the seeds to create division; so people would harm each other as he wishes. So let us make sure his wishes don't come to fruition.

To The Lord

I would like that the real snatch and grab is to get to know you better than ever. They can snatch and grab the love you have waiting on them from out of the air in front of you. Therefore the safety of the people has been heard by the Lord and now you can hear from the Lord with all the love you let me give.

We should never humiliate a culture!

Check this out whether it may be right or questionable. If an officer has a body camera on them and a shooting occurs and harms someone. If they were trained up the right way and release spiritual operation as what may be taking place with this book talking them through it. Can we see this as the extra measure of love for everybody to stop and prevent any bad thing from happening.

The Big Problem

A lot of the work has been done because people do not want to do the hard work that it takes to get along with others. Learning what it takes to not get along is the hardest part and that is what I have done and it was not easy. One of the first things I have done is learning what can be done on both sides then learn what the Lord says about it all. That comes from mankind's first experience with God and then each other.

People need to read more

Therefore, this tool can make a difference in the response the officer has in a life and death matter. Are they better off with it than without it? I believe so. This teaches people that sin can work against and through them and how to help stop it.

To break it down it can't be known unless it is known to say no to it. Give up all of the unclaimed ghosts that you won't have that you can be free of; now and forever.

I thank God he is allowing me to keep my hands on the plow to bring in the harvest to feed the people and to help change the course of history in the people on earth to make it better for everyone.

Thank you from Bro. Bush your servant and this I say from the bottom and top of my heart. Therefore don't let the Lord give it and you throw it away; life. I thank the Lord for the work I do that comes out of the body of Christ to grow love and create jobs.

To now say that things could have been worse in the way the police have acted toward the people might not sound as good as it should but it could work in the same manner of which the people act toward the police so to not point fingers at anyone is where we should be to start off new.

As A Fact

Additional measures of thought could be a part of the problem like it was back in wartime when even the black soldiers were so mistreated and abused by the white soldiers. At night black soldiers shot at their own soldiers because of the hate they were made to have for them. Then it had gotten so bad they had to have intervention to help end it through a higher ranking person.

Is this a part of the past sins of the fathers that added to a flaw in the law. If it had anything to do with the civil right movement also we can bury the past dead influence we have also by way of a new age prescription of love. This may be something that police who were soldiers can give a thought about.

We can shun all darkness that wants to walk into the future with us. You can live the right side up to stop a spiritual illness that has been a plague in the past.

There is a better chance to plan the seed of progress in the less heated time of the year since most of the problems occur in the summer time months. This way we can have a step on the problem to out-step it to leave it in the past. If we save one it is what matters.

Personally

I think that the rallies and marches have helped make people more aware and have awakened the conscious of American about this issue. I believe this did a lot of good.

Now I implore you to get the word out about this new way to even more help. One reason why now can this almost knock the edge off of people wanting to harm the police because it explains to them the problem and takes the problem to a place where people don't or should not go with themselves to do anyone harm that can be prevented as a cure or deterrent otherwise.

If the brain can catch a thought at 268 hundred miles an hour, how much do we miss?

It is time to lose the "jacked up" sense of protect and serve.

Family

It is hard to be able to see someone who misses out on a growing up moment.

GST

This is the real selfie and close up. It can also be called the icing on the cake but I will say it is the ice for your tea that has been made in the winter season or in the cold for your use during the summer and or hot time of the year to always be able to keep it cool because it is no fun when anyone acts like a rabbit with a gun. So drink of this cool water or tea. The ice is on me says the Lord. You make the tea (Teaching eternal advancement).

No one needs to be in the sea of a ball of confusion about this issue any longer.

To Be Clear

This is a two-way street for people to come together and it doesn't have a racial barrier. So all are allowed in, to help end the senseless harm (whatever kind) that can be thought of, or taken against, anybody people, police.

This is a part of The new and better summertime ahead so keep your head cool.

For the Ambassadors: It's Time to Cut the Cake of Ice
GST

If it is ice, you don't need a Zamboni just a pair of ice skates. Try it, I did and when I fell, I got up.

It has been time to stop going oops upside your own head because of the lack of facts for our defense against Satan. The completion of the beginning of wisdom starts with this first step to add to what you know now. Therefore, I will take an outlook as if you completed this assignment. You have earned a degree or diploma for a life and some spiritual skill.

Police officers wearing cameras and even first aid care are now available for them to use in their jobs. Therefore, why not use all avenues, including spiritual skills.

Everyone that should want to be a part of this process of growth out of a part of the dark age is in one (or more) of these four groups: 1. Police; 2. People who want to harm them; 3. Those who are dissatisfied with them; and 4. Those who are curious to know what is happening.

The pain that people have is due to one way most of the time, they don't have the Godly skills needed to deal with or subdue as if it is a juggling act, with sin as a ball of some kind until it falls. to stop the act and pain to stop it to where it seems unbearable with the fact the Lord loves you.

It is hard to know, share and be a part of the truth when someone is in so much pain. It is hard to see right from wrong when doing it no matter what someone has or gets out of the act they may commit. That is what we all are to be trying to fix it from the top down.

What may be the biggest pain not teaching why there is pain and how to not let it hurt you to a point where it can destroy you or someone else and not making the opportunities to outgrow it, with love school, jobs, a future, etc.

Cynicism is or could be the lack of love and trust in mankind and the Lord that some people don't know about that leaves them in the void-noid avenue of life.

This part of life that we are talking about is something we can have and   it will come later if you live long enough. So don't rush into it, let it flow into you. It may seem like a now though for later.

Time for the new "flat foot" bring this to a beginning one thing left to do is first learn to become a Good Samaritan with a friendly way of helping.

No One Never Need to Think
in Line With Though of An Uncertain Future

If we don't see who we are we still need to know we are whomever we are any way and a way always comes out of no way in life to grow to the right way to go eventually.

We can keep a miracle by giving it away.

Don't go into people's gates of intellect without knowing you are going there.

We have to develop a new sensitive way of thinking about others who are not of the same minority as we may be. This information can help to do that by teaching people to become color blind to everything by justice. It also helps to have more of the same people who have come from the same culture in the community where the race card cannot be played.

The Wisdom of a Tool to Know

Therefore, get the skills to stop it; this ounce of prevention is for you.

Why do police officers shoot when they don't have to? A possible answer could be the sin nature or a mental deficiency that creates fear for self or hatred for others that is in them. Where does sin nature come from? Being lost, blind, or not having the right relationship with the Lord.

Now is the time to run to glory, not from it

My Biggest Concern

Is not your earthly body but your heavenly presence?

Time Out

Did you hear the bells ring? The thing we can learn is like having an officer present with no bullies.

A Melting Pot

The new rainbow of people that one day will be thankful they mix together. How to find a new way of making a living that will help the multitudes. Spiritual skills enriches your imagination to bring about ideas that fill in the parts of life that are or may be needed or missing to create hope the commerce of love that include money to live off of, plus new resources that help people sustain.

Have we studied enough to head off the problems of the future today if not we can? The new books I will be introducing can help to give the much needed wisdom to help people study to show them self-approved, by knowing what is going on, on the new levels that are truly old.

It is Not New News

The Lord wants to take his people to a different level if they want to go. Time to get ready or not it is coming to the Earthly life we all live with, the stopping and tearing down of the spiritual will of humanity that harms life, property and the living conditions we love.

They say there is nothing richer than teaching. If I were to obtain the right to do that to also have to lose out on worldly wealth, then let it be, I would be a teacher first. Now the time has changed for me to work within the system of profit that has to come with love.

Let's Stop

We can help stop the aftermath of issues before they occurred in a new presence of a better sprit we share.

No weapons formed against me shall prosper does not mean that no weapons will be formed against me. It means that the weapons formed against me will not be successful by the will of the lord.

What Strike Are You in need to get off of to make it home?

1. Void-noid the lost and confused and the not being trained up right, that can step in to some kind of fox-hole as if they should and then shouldn't.

2. Towerism the power that goes to the head and the ego leads the heart in lots of ways that can be stopped.

3. Sin-nature last stop to not see it as a fall because of the non-acceptance of Christ the right way or do we close our eyes with the law so not to see the space between use and the lord ?

To know these things give a freedom to you that listen. Becoming trained up is where you are to avoid the holds to not fall in or wants to be in just to feel something even if it is some kind of pain; then to lose it because your sin-nature wants others to feel it also. What happens without it? Foolishness, strife, fear, etc. It comes from the lack of love that you can have to lose it.

The biases that we all have some time deep down inside can be stopped from becoming a part of us at a drop of a hat, once we take off the hat that can't be seen that is made out of rat hair.

The way things were at first in Selma Alabama that had that had a reflection on young that has become a part of today it is bad and no telling how many were trapped in a tower that went to a hellish reunion in that part of life for them. Do we as people need the shame that shows up that day at the bridge? Also the shame that shows up in hellish ways that we can't see but some go there, who deserves too?

We have seen the things we don't need to be repeating in history: the people wanting to fight back; the people getting harmed; the people harming others that are wrong for it.

How do we get things done?

If we understand what manna is and the nourishment it can provide in a realm of spirituality, then we should know that the people of Egypt understood what God's hand meant. It meant one thing, love, but so many are lost on the other factors that take place between the point of love and the point of what you have created and have no alternative but to expect. Therefore, giving witness to this understanding the people of Egypt knew not the same thing that Moses did because Moses knew the Lord's heart.

If mankind knows the fact that anyone following the Lord's law will be put on trial sometimes by mankind he can endure it. But if they don't know the laws of man they can't know the laws of the Lord. This has a one-way street that can be understood very simply. Man can sacrifice his life for what is right and live forever in eternity. Sometimes mankind feels he must take a licking and act like a chicken.

Now is the time to clear the chickens out of the barnyard before they go to a real court of law, not just one mankind has made up. Forget about the fake get with what is real and let your love shine beyond the gravestone you may perceive to exist in your life before your time.

In life, we get used and abused but that doesn't make us a fool!

Who is willing to leave one more level of another kind of darkness behind? It is I to my Lord with thanks to thee!

Rebuilding trust is a part of being a Samaritan

To avoid the void-noid can be completed by growing with the Lord

I like people to show what they know sometimes and not tell me

Sin nature has a division of mental deficiency that creates fear for self or health but spiritual skills can give it the heart treatment plan to clear up a possible mental lapse.

Some of the good news

Has the fact of the new camera system on the job gotten harder because police are being watched and can be held accountable for their actions that can be witnessed by others and to not upset the ground floor it has become so much of a mishap we as a nation can't afford this alien alternative in our land any more, just for doing a job and making a mistake due to their fear by letting some people drive off and get away as was done in a incident.

I can't perceive this happening but it can out of fear. That is what you get away from when you know what you can do to make life better for you and everybody on all sides of your wisdom to bring this to a better understanding? You can't, fear your job that may makes you under do your job and now you don't have to overdo it either. You can keep things and your time balanced and that is what it is all about no pressure at all from within our mind and heart.

This information gives people the power to deal with what can be seen and what can't be seen within them to make them able to stop more things from going wrong on their job when making a split decision about an action to take. To also never get into a wolf pack mentality like back in the day giving resolution to our growth in a non-bias time of a different state of mind that is trying to keep up with the spirit, the old police force of Selma, Alabama, or as was done recently in a car pursuit in Cleveland, Ohio. Now you can stay on the right track on a one on one level of thought process and not get stuck there by yourselves. That causes some to do the wrong thing by going along with the crowd and we can thank God for this break that affects the soul through the misguided spirit that some people have no matter who they are or what they do. It is his power of love he has for us to teach us his will, to love one another daily on all levels of life, with his power to love us as we should love one another in all kinds of trouble.

We can de-traumatize our society with the wisdom that creates hope with an "us" program as this one as a crime stopper so we can cut the percentage way down including offers of the law that have filling also.

Spiritual physics: could what I have been called to write about be name this? Additionally, can we see through darkness? Yes, with the light of the Lord and without it do we fall into it and then not accept it out of our lack of wisdom.

This is not that hard to do the phase of using the parliamentary procedures that the Lord has for us once we have the know-how.

One of the roughest things I had to learn about some people is once they get set in their ways and have a so-called security blanket of whatever kind they will refuse to learn something new until something bad may happen in or around their life.

One of the reasons the world is in the shape it is in is people don't want to teach the things we all need to learn and too many people are too busy toy shopping and joy popping. Stop it if it is causing a part of the people and the world to become harmed.

People can control and stop a lot of the "whys," "whats," "whens," "wheres" and "hows" by knowing what is real. Time to trade in "what nots" for the "know what this book has made known to you."

My suggestion is people need to stop sitting on a rotten egg. If this is you, learn to become a real hero. If there are any stones left that need to be turned over, please do so. What is left out of this equation is not all up to me you get my meaning I hope.

This work is not a put down but a get up, pick up and stay up. For what you need to do that is right! It is important to have the exploration of a curious mind inside of one's self.

This May Sound Like a Harvey Wall banger

That is a kind of wake-up call to know there are sicknesses on a carnal level of life that bring fear to people. There also can be sicknesses on a spiritual level that some people would really fear and not want to identify with. But if it can be explained there may be even more skepticism about this at first because you never heard of it. So don't kick it to the curb because it may be just what the doctor ordered. Even if it sounds like it came from some kind of quack doctor. Now as I said before, don't hate the message you, you might need it. Now take a breath and go have a laugh and tell a good joke to keep thing good every time you think they are not.

The releasing of the tension can be done once we understand how at times we are not fighting against one another but with principalities and authorities of darkness between oneself and others by proxy. The thief uses people as pawns in his presence of a dead spirit sin-drome to steal, kill and/or destroy and use the people to tower up to keep the fight going to not free the rights of the people.

I am not trying to scare or spook anyone, but it was said by one of the founders of the constitution without God in it, the running of the newly founded country of America will not work as expected like people hope basically and we don't allow the present thought of the Lord in the government or the operation of it. I suggest the process of a mistake may be made out of a bad spiritual spirit that some people have in them and that includes anyone, also police officers.

You can protect yourself by learning about it. That way you can avoid a problem just in case because if you do harm someone and you should not have done it and it is on camera you will go to jail.

This is a part of the past and it hasn't been fixed or repaired all the way in all the areas that it has been broken in and the justice system may not have a long way to go. We see that in the prison system and the injustices on the inmates or the people of color that are locked up. We don't need to focus on this when we can and need to fix this one problem. First off what could be an inner fight that someone may have and it is harming others, whether they are a criminal or not.

To go off the beaten path, is it a change that the spirit of mankind that has no light that was killed in the past such as the blacks who were killed and hanged are affecting some people who have not been protected to cause them a spiritual sickness that is still being spread to others and it could have an effect on all people the police or the people who commit the crimes better known as sin. I don't know but if so we all can get the freedom from this with the power of light that comes from the Lord.

It is my hope that the people who work within the justice system will also be aware of any problems they may have who locked up people for a crime an treat them wrong as if there is some kind of chain gang mentally they have that add on time to their sentence for the hell of it.

Do you think the people you work for need to pay for this? I don't think so. Is this fiction or non-fiction? It is up to you to decide.

This treasure was created by the will of the father therefore don't think it is just mankind's word which has holes in them at times. Rely on the Lord to make it right.

Believe This

To make note, I am not one who believes in the practice of any kind of voodoo or hoodoo stuff that I can't make sense out of.

This is Not Totally Obvious Information
(that some of the public doesn't
want to know about but it can save lives)

Break it Down to Clean This Up

Hate crimes are sin crimes that come from people with sin-nature that we all are born with, to stop the process we are to remember we are supposed to be the righteousness of

Christ that can wash away sin-nature. Once we receive him we are washed by the blood that he shed on the cross. If we have hate in us and say we are in the presence with him we lie to ourselves.

We can be thankful we all can become cavaliers.

There are still things that are one of a kind and can't be duplicated or replaced when you keep something pure and simple and real; it is love.

We don't want to dry up a spiritual well that gives life sustenance of love when we look to know about our silver lining in our lifetime. Now look what can happen with a little ingenuity and forethought. From an accident sometimes comes a miracle to complete a part of the Lord in us.

We Can't

Afford to become a target risk for Satan.

Everyone

Everyone, at some time, needs someone to dump a bucket of proof right over their heads. The best way this is done is by you doing it yourself.

A Call for the Facts

We must know of the ways of employment on the new level of how to succeed. Therefore, as an individual leader we must be in agreement with an unwritten policy that entitles you a catalyst in the right perspective to see others for better than they present themselves at times.

Ousting

Dismissing all of the bleep thoughts by bleeping them out. They try to register but they should not have one or more times to try being placed somewhere before it disappears.

1. Salvation is deliverance prosperity to include your wealth and healing things from the past with love for today.

The development of learning can become somewhat a level of principles to grow into with this book.

We Can Stop

A spiritual parasite named Satan without religion. If an officer has a problem in the first place it doesn't help them in their work but with this new help it can make it better for all.

If I Could I Should

Can I not say something, one thing that helps to bring justice to the people where there seems like no justice. Complete this book and comment on it out loud so all can hear.

A part of what this book is all about is to develop a new moral attitude for an approach to all people saintly and those who may be lacking a part of their sanity along with the mentally challenged to gain the insight to use the spiritual skill gifts that we all have attested in life that lessen the harm we do to others if in the wrong situation and to ourselves if any at all.

How Can I Be Sure

This wisdom gives the insight that creates a way to tap into spiritual intervention that can be a better way of having a tool that works which money can't buy. What do you do with the people of fear who are about to lose their life with or about the way they are approached by others? Something you can't do a thing about but a good spirit can do everything to stop the ungodliness from setting in that give a freedom to realize the fear in others and the fear that some may have of what to expect of themselves; more so to know a calm sea of love is there no matter how things look.

Who says this process will work for everyone? Not I but some may get out of it more than they may ever know in one way or you can get out what you put in. End a problem before it becomes one. Now who has the best look at this new level of non-stinking thinking? You do; or do you?

There is no police officer that I believe is in any department they work for across the country that may state an officer will have to read and study a manual as this one. That is why I personally thank you for your presence in this way of learning something different and new on your own that you may never get an order from a commanding officer to read.

I also have a book that may add more to your personal campaign to make life better on not just your job but life. This book helps people accept to learn more of the Lord's intervention. The title is _The New Added Protection for the Development of Teens and Young Adults at Risk_. Now this may also help you to understand teenagers and young adults better.

The other book I will refer to will help you develop spiritual skills to create God's intervention that is or can be put in your presence by the will of the Lord working in you in a supernatural way. The book is entitled _All Peoples Handbook_. This will be something that will give you some direction for life circumstances as your faith grows.

I am not trying to present more of the books at BTHPM as a promotion but this knowledge can be found in more than one book, that we all can learn to walk down into our spirit to keep all safe and teach each other the ways to think in order to live and let live. No prejudice ever entered into the words I write to you.

Is this America on one level that has gone
wrong in one way but not in another

No it is not okay but the team player, football, baseball, hockey or basketball, all have a somewhat wolf pack mentality but it is not right either and they get find when police get it too but in another way it gets people harmed. But now we are thinking of a better approach that could be used next time this wolf pack mentality tries to come upon someone. This may be up to you and you know who you are if you need a different level to help you refrain from this kind of action.

Know How to Avoid Train Wrecks that Satan Causes

It is somewhat known that when more than enough goes into a somewhat war state of a fight there is a somewhat loss of control as if too many cooks spoil the broth and a calamity occur on a wolf pack mentality that makes trouble for some on an invisible level at first with a price that should not have to be paid. The Lord tells you how to fight and win. This is a key to independently becoming virtuous.

To get all the breakdowns to stop something from happening, read the books to learn how to stop it. Start a new you!

The Un-harm We Can Do

The last presence that I don't want to impress on you is do more black men want the white people to kill them than the people of their own skin color, because of the black on black crime in the USA. I can't say can anyone because it is not good in every way.

This Syllabus is for the Personal Development of a Better Kind of Life

Don't be someone who takes something apart trying to fix it, then put it back together broken.

The police can help stop the scathing that takes place in society today

It is possible that man can't put a charge and/or conviction on someone who the Lord can charge and/or convict? It was meant in the past for some to only be convicted by the Lord in sentencing. Did they get convicted, the slave owner, by the laws of the Lord? I believe that, since they "claimed" it was legal because they wrote the law as they wrote lots of treaty and broke them.

Take Note

Now what can we rely on? Not the justice system all of the time to get to the bottom line that can be looked at as revenge and mankind does this to try to punish someone for taking the wholeness from others whether it is time in jail and or money. But it doesn't happen all of the time but revenge is mine says the Lord and he will make you whole one day if you don't know it.

There are some people who have gotten away with breaking mankind's laws, who have been working in conjunction with the void-noid sin-drome, and think it is normal. They are somewhat linked up with it and they think they can do anything and get away with it. don't fool yourself; you are better off paying a debt to society for your wrong doings than paying a debt to Satan for following his principles that lead to darkness for an eternity.

To All

May you know a part of all of thee people can stop the feelings of regret for some of their actions. This will hopefully help people stop thinking someone gets away with something. No one gets away with the wrong they do.

In saying all of this try to always keep peace in your heart.

You Can

Prejudge a man any way you want but you will never know the soul of his spirit. So why be facetious about others.

At Birth

Be a part of the amazing things coming to and out of your life.

Get Connected to Know Harmony

What could be most people's biggest fear? It is getting to the next us. These factors can help stop the fear once you know them. We do fear what we don't know and/or how to believe in it sometimes, can and will or will not affect us.

Whose News

Do good people make bad mistakes? Yes therefore protect yourself from the sin-nature that all people have even though some are protected and others are not. Be not one who is shy of the truth that self is not perfect.

Is it time for as many or all police officers of all kinds, state patrol officers, highway patrols also, to learn to add more insurance of a different kind to their life. No one needs to have their life put in a bad way because of the lack of love that is understanding reasoning and the power to stop themselves and know it.

Who is, or may be, the hardest person for some people to get along with? It may be you and lots of people don't know it so they blame it on others. Therefore we go along with the fact it is others we can't get along with to make ourselves feel okay.

Now if we are always dead set on helping solve someone else's problems and we need to first start with ourselves. Put the sin-nature in its place as needed, it is a part of the art of surviving together with all others.

There are needs some people have
that may be one thing: spiritual growth

Keep in mind and know no matter what you do for a living. The Lord's is not a respecter of persons. Therefore, you are equal in his sight, because he wants us all to do well.

The people that have a greater faith in life, can have it all!

No One Need to be Knocked

There is one big thing that people should stop doing; judging people by what they have and do and to not knock them at all per stereotyping.

In the USA we are the new possibility to help lead the world

To help, this is spiritual execution to execute in this new day. The wisdom within includes another side. 1. If you get enough exercise physically to help relieve stress, etc. this is the way to get the spiritual exercise you may need to help change and fix a problem you may not know you have.

The Free Ounce of Love

Something I will say about this work is, it is not hard to swallow. It is easy to digest to help stop people from continuing to do the void noid things. I have been planting seeds since the beginning of my spiritual growth to show others how to plant their own.

I treat people like flowers and watch them bloom. This kind of trip can be a great world travel though if we look at the writing I do, it is like a worldly love affair. Now can this writing stand the test of time? I ask myself as if I have a somewhat untamed spirit.

I Do

There are not too many presents that I have been given in my past for me to carry to the future so I leave them with all.

Now to really go off the beaten path does some who are killed by others have a dead soul sin-drome that makes it seem like they have a death wish and does it attract the people who have a sin-nature to do the job of killing. Does it sounds sick and if it is in anyway somewhat real, it is of a satanic sickness but it too may exist and I do talk about it in one of my other books I helped to write. But could the black or Afro American rather die at the hand of a white person as was in the days of slavery because of being tied to the past in a dark way?

If that is the case do some white people prefer to kill them in a way they can't explain? This we may never know to its fullest extent but if it is real, we do need help from the Lord. That is when the part of some blacks wanting whites to kill them and they taunt them into doing it.

Now is there also an underlying suicide issue and do they want to become some kind of martyr of some kind?

More History that stop a issues

In the past harm that was done to a lot of black people was out of hatred and fear of what they may become if we let them think they are equal to all kinds of people. Now today it is a fear of being hurt by them more so, if I don't stop them in almost any way I can. But this too can come to an end. But the black people will have to have a part in stopping this too.

Do we, as humans, have a part of the sin of the forefathers stuck to us and if so we too can become free from them.

There it is

There is one thing that people must do on both sides and if they can't this book might not give you the light we all seek in one way or another it is trusting the people who you may have an issue against you may not want to but if you have the attitude of I don't want to trust and it is not because you can't and you just won't I offer you one other way pray to receive what you are in need of because this may not be it. Then remember if you think you are lonely it is not true so get to know who might not see the real you.

To Note the Present

If the frame we put ourselves in has a state of being that reflect on towerism in a certain kind of people that can be found in the part of the past in our times that present the same ways as Ferguson with the system on both levels with a reflection of Selma, AL that happened to be one of the sweetest sounds I know. Now we are still on the march for freedom and we hopefully won't have to go any further to get this problem out of our lifetime.

The towers that fell down and resigned from the jobs because they let the abuse of justice become a part of the egotistical level of thinking under there witch that is barbaric and was displayed by their law enforcement procedures that need to change also.

The black man who may be the hidden shooter that happened lately in Ferguson, Missouri is nowhere near being an American we as black people when the time for freedom came we went to the face of people and not in the black darkness to challenge anyone when we were fed up. If this was a black person then there is a hell-of-a curse on them because it has never been in our nature to be that way as if we were a sniper of some kind. In retrospect, this could have been anyone who shot the police officers; a white man or even another officer of the law who may have had a grudge as some did have in the past when they killed their own, or did an outsider come in to cause trouble for people trying to start another riot to have more people harmed. No one needs to commit a cowardly act in life. Now that we may know who may have committed the crime can we be sure at this time until the facts are in on the one that did it? God only knows.

By learning these things in this book and dealing with them on a spiritual level of thinking and not a carnal or earthly way someone who has this kind of problem, it too can help stop the "maniactivity" over something that is not worth it. Therefore, don't harass one's self once you are friend with yourself in the light of glory.

A Beginning for All

The gift of clear vision takes tenacity and a pure heart to soar above the clouds in spiritual delight.

One of the worse things Satan could ever steal from anyone is their children's heart

We can also share the trip to a place as the Iditarod race, without being in the cold.

Know Now You Can

Find the common thread in you to knit a blanket of trust for you to share.

Know that love done right can change the world

You do need to fear the devil and know he is no joke when you don't know the Lord. But the foolish do not and the "know it alls" are who he wants. My advice is, don't become a non-mystic about this.

Come Get

Some of the tools out of God's tool chest as if it is a part of the presence of the Lord in his Ark of the Covenant for you.

Yes

I felt better yesterday than I felt the day before.

This is a Plan the Lord has Given Me for Us

A Plan to Stop the Negative Development
of People and Their Bad Influences

The Big Ones and Little Ones With A New Kind of Love

Heaven is Watching Our Tomorrows

Have we studied enough to head off the problems of the future today? The new books I will be introducing can help to give the much needed wisdom to help people study to show themselves approved, by knowing what is going on, on the new levels that are truly old.

We have picked other books to highlight to help the people of the world to not fear the coming of daily trouble and save them from themselves to let the Lord save them from a real living kind of hell on Earth or otherwise.

There is An Escape Plan Put in Place

It is Not New News

The Lord wants to take his people to a different level if they want to go. Time to get ready or not it is coming to the Earthly life we all live.

This work is like a homeland security program to teach a new kind of respect and love for Americans within a home study course to do the repairs wherever it is needed that has been developed by the Lord just for the USA, to start off first. Then others may use the new kind of blessings. This way of leverage we get two things done, one fix what could have been a problem and head it off or stop it. To uncover what may be covered in the darkness of youth and some adults to help them to stop on the right track, which stops the tearing down of the spiritual will of humanity and humanness that harms life, property and the living conditions that we as a people destroy in a state of youth that tear down the very cities we live in so the past won't repeat itself of destruction and rioting.

There should be a bill put forth to the legislators to never let a youth play with any type of gun that looks like a real weapon in their possession. If this bill does not pass, it should still become legislation in the hearts of all parents toward their children.

What may be one of people's biggest problems with harming one another? Could it be someone is being lost in a spiritual warfare and may not have known it? People have to learn the right way to fight spiritual wars and not to include a human fight.

The fact is that if someone is in a spiritual fight with Satan within themselves and someone comes along and there is a misunderstanding. They may take it out on them and do them harm by making a molehill out of a mountain, that leaves some people in a black zone that kills people from them feeling trapped and not knowing how to get down out of a trap as some people are trapped in a self-built tower of some kind and don't know how to get down out of the darkness of the non-physical side of the fight that only the Lord has the right to fight for you. Now are the people in towers fighting Satan to get down out of them (some are and others are not), until it falls on them or someone else who may be innocent? Some people get caught in the crossfire of violence because of this and there is freedom from this to be used.

Let's Stop

We can help stop the aftermath of issues before they occur

Welcome too A Cleansing of the Spiritual Nature time

A cleansing of the spiritual nature time has come even if it goes back one year or one thousand years or more. Thanks to the Lord for new starts daily

The effects of the past that have some people held captive in the present day can and will be erased with spiritual skills to stop the harm that it can do if you feel you are trapped in it whether your people were doing the harm or harmed by it.

Fix It

By whatever means necessary from the passions or feelings it has now risen up to a not just black thing but an American thing to repair the problem.

Do

Get faithful over a few things
and get out of everyone else's business

Know that no one has to be anyone else's scapegoat.

These are the words to hang onto. I like to think I have fulfilled my loyalties to the Lord. As a man knowing we are still breaking off from a piece of Selma to get more of the freedom the Lord promised me away from sin.

This is Not a Paradox; it is an epiphany

M-N

You are in good hands when you know who is sharing the best hand with you about life.

Use the power of a true spirit to level the feeling of love in and of life. re-define your sensitivity. Have the sensitivity rebirth of life in it all.

It may seem a little ironic but police and military personnel can be one of the main level of people to benefit from spiritual skills since they are somewhat watch people for the world and the security in general for all also the unlisted soldiers who become police officers.

There are good people everywhere doing every kind of job. Let's celebrate them even if we don't know them along with praying that the lost get found to save their salvation.

Prepare to never fall into the gray spirit sin-drome. As we people may get the gray sky sickness from not enough sunshine and our bodies could use more. Get in all the spiritual food you can.

Now could this be an old cliché don't just be the long hand of the law but the long hand of the Lord. Does your mindset fix things before they are broken? If not, then change the thinking to know no so you don't do the things that may trouble you for or in life.

Now there is a difference in the wolf pack mentalities. There are some that are not good and there are some that are good woof packs that share in a brotherhood that wants to solve problems and issues in life with friendship.

I am one of many or a few who have discovered the mystery of the keys to spiritual nature and ways to develop the right growth patterns.

To receive empowerment of greatness within you must display one factor. It is to have unconditional love for the people who want you to get set off track in life. It doesn't mean to become foolish for anyone but let them know you have it and it is real. Then mark and make the factors that store it in your heart. To tell them show them but not to let them hurt you or misuse you. It is the way that the Lord left here for us to become like him; thanks to Him and his love for you.

A New York police officer went to a level the void-noid but came out because it is not only a "black thing," it is a "we thing" if at all.

Could this book put a new twist on the judgment of the police thinking and instead of the problem getting out of hand because something they feel they cannot do they should get out of the way so the Lord can do his thing to show his love. Therefore if we let it go we will rely on the Lord to do his job and if we do see the wrong result we know it came out right.

In the past and the future we don't have time to fight a fight that the Lord got. So if you are not aware of who you are and what you are and what you are doing and call yourself grown, don't fool yourself even if I maybe and others are fooled by you.

To the Innocent

We can believe that someone can lead a lot of others in the right ways to lead.

One thing

There is one thing I try to do with all of the writings is put forth the effort of having the best part of the saving grace of the Lord in us.

Who Knows

That in the depths of darkness in the farthest reaches of the mind in a black hole of the forefathers, that causes some police officers get stuck dumbfounded in their actions of apprehending someone and have a master mentality that says to them if you cannot do exactly what I said I will harm you as if you were a slave and they were a slave owner.

Now if this is a need still for some to be treated for it is there for been treated and you are the most real from it whose faith is it the unnecessary harm that some face. If the child is not trained up right, could it be the adult in their life? and if the adult in their life wasn't either, there is one or more people who may be at fault, a friend, a butcher a baker a candlestick maker the preachers, teachers or shepherds of life.

I say this because if the love of the Lord is to be shared all over the world, then we are not sharing it as it was meant to be. Therefore, it is time to be greater with sharing so there won't be excuses or someone don't have to be on trial twice because of not knowing the difference between mankind's laws and the Lord's laws in order for them to not be convicted twice for the same crime, even if they get unlucky and get off for the crime down on earth but not upon their intent to enter heaven.

Therefore, I say don't be one who don't observe the day of the Lord's resurrection because it meant you can be resurrected too. So stay out of the lost land with being indicted on the crime you didn't commit but you did commit it by a way of being a proxy for Satan.

Note

There are similar paragraphs within some of my books that I need to use to express a point, like a parable with information that comes with scriptures that may be repeated in writing to take you to a greater understanding but by no means are the complete messages the same in any books but the one for you to adopt the spiritual skills needed in a specific manner.

There is a collaboration of thinking that leads the way in my work. It has the right to be placed in more than one book that helps to clear up a point of light that may be on another level that uses a part of the wisdom to see a different reward.

The crazy part of towerism is when a group of people gather and are on a kind of natural high and a team loses the one game that means it all the championships. The idea is not to be a sore loser, which should be the normal reaction, but the fans and some team members do not because they are in the void-noid and it is innocence but the trouble is not a justified a way to act the right way do I need to say more so end this chapter but there is more to learn from.

Now it is like a tower affect that sneaks up on you and it causes some of you to lose it. Now were you on some kind of border anyway? Therefore if it needs more it is the preparation plan for spiritual skills that can help end this way of life.

The Offsetting of an Officer

He had been led with an uncontrollable unnatural sickness humans can't do a thing about that is of a somewhat Satanic process in people in a situation where the wolf-pack mentality somewhat takes control over them, even though he may somewhat lead all others who are just as guilty as sin. Could I see my way of helping someone in that position? Yes, but I don't know how to help but the Lord does.

Take Notice

There are three different levels of the wolf-pack mentality. The first is the lone wolf who doesn't need anyone to join in with them but it is extreme for them to shoot someone in the back. The next is the leader of the wolf-pack mentality. They get caught up with others who follow them. They too are prone to go overboard. The last is the follower who has no sense of the use of their own leadership when following someone else, even if they know it is wrong. Now what level do you fit in and if you don't know then are you protected from the void-noid or not?

Are some white law enforcement officers still stuck on the inside with madness because they hate there is no more slavery as it was two hundred years ago. They don't know it because they have to be a part of working in the field to stop a black person from doing something wrong if they are or not.

Do some officers of the law need to see the history of a people that they may need to know better? If they do I think they may need to take a trip to the state of South Carolina. This may help bring some resolution to their issues to take them away from the higher percentage and lower the percentage of hurt, harm and danger from 7-10 to 1-3 or lower, to help keep them safe from themselves.to find a place to know more about this understanding take a trip to the land of the free plantation museum state of Louisiana.

Time for some people to stop playing the inner anger game that they may not know they are playing that can harm them. It is like having your back turn on yourself and you don't know it, even though you play it out loud when you are around your own race of people, it may catch up with you one day. It is wonderful to know how right it feels to see and do right about this all the time.

My Sight Gets Weak for You

If the division of two equals the wrong side of one, then there is no way to understand the consequences as if a man in the service came out that had the void-noid on the outsiders of the actions. Then the change is not aware of and come out in the new position of an officer then the outcome may be the same the wisdom I write that I do not even understand but I know it comes from love.

You Have Been Foretold

Some may consider this as a warning that the essential facts surrounding spiritual skills are for the development of many presents of growth. One of the first is to let all people know that you are to apply the necessary tools to your life personally in order for you to bypass the death in the grave.

The consequences of that rely upon your obedience in the will of God. The spiritual skills principles are to be developed with an understanding that you must gird your loins due to one major fact; you will be able to knock down all strong holds that Satan may have on you and you will have to confront him yourself because he will have to come down out of the high places where he has declared his strong holds to meet with you personally.

Now your preparation relies upon you because you are not perfect and the flaw that you may have due to the sin nature that has been put on you at birth will and is looked over by the Lord but Satan will try to rely upon that if you are not girded up to spread it upon you as a cancer to bring about death of your spirit.

We all stumble as was when the people of Israel came out of bondage but due to them not being prepared as the Lord wished, it took them time to reach the Promised-land and they had to go through the process of eliminating the cancer that affecting their spirit.

Spiritual skills can and will bring about a better presence of the gifts we all have been blessed with, but it is up to us to allow ourselves to be baptized in the Spirit. There are so many who are afraid of being baptized in the water. Therefore it really gives them an excuse to fear being baptized in the Spirit even more.

As for me, the biggest fear I ever had in my life was when the Paraklètos and me were in the presence of Satan who came to kill, steal and destroy me in my sleep. There was a loud bellowing noise that came out of my mouth that scared the hell out of me and I knew it was done that I was endorsed, indoctrinated and called to bring forth the wisdom to supply others to lead them to the Promised-land within so they could survive on the earthly land that we live upon.

I spread this message of hope that is created by the good news to not fear the gift that the Lord gives but before you can receive an anointing or a gift you have to be born in it with it or receive it and it shall not come to pass until you are baptized in the spirit. If you want to know what the Lord has for you to do in the body of Christ, you must become baptized in the spirit. Therefore fear not the presence of who you are but embrace it with love. Move forward and as you are confronted possibly daily, know that the armor of the Lord protects you at all costs even though you may have to proceed through pain and misery your eternal well-being has been prepared to protect you. This is the greatest message I can share with you.

Don't fear the water, you won't get burnt. If you do, you may get two for one: being sterilized.

This may be a bonus that gives us an opportunity to stop so many individuals from taking their gifts to the grave. It also may be on a level where the Lord may spare many before he comes back within a small (or large) measure of time in order for others to get their houses in order. We must pray to see these days made new for a multitude of people who are lost out of the body of Christ.

By Unpopular Vote

This country has been suppressing God on almost every level of duty in our work place and the love he has for us and that is the reason why there are so many wounded individuals who are losing their eternal wellbeing due to the strong holds that Satan has been controlling. The new movement of spiritual skills is to free individuals from this bondage. To help free the people without them becoming lost in the wilderness we are certifying this indictment that the powers that rule in high places in darkness will fall before mankind before the end of time as we know it.

What Can be Said to People

Don't be like the scorpion that wanted to cross the river. A frog took him upon his back and the scorpion gave the impression he would not sting the frog. Half way across it stung the frog and knew he would die but said it is in my nature. That can be represented in a way that doesn't harm us when we are the sons and daughters in the body of Christ.

To Have Flowers Blossomed For You

To share spiritual skills will correct the incorrect that has a badge of horror that mankind has not placed on them and can't be touched or removed by them, has a fulfillment that is like no other. How would I know if I didn't care?

I, Too

I have to come to terms with myself and I thank God I have family, some that are of my blood and some who are not, to help keep me standing upward.

A Good Use of Us

This topic is in no way new, it is not a phenomenon it is a new touch of reality to be shared and used.

To Know II

I have seen something that was terrifying in a humble spirit that was an awakening of who I could have been that doesn't please me but I carry on.

The Last Stronghold of an Unseen Sickness

Could there be a legion of blindness that affects some police officers and they don't know about it that has come from the ancestors of the past that gives them a thought of I am not prejudice at the conscious level of thought but at the subconscious state of mind. There are issues that affect them in a way that leaves them open to fall into a dark side of an interaction that can harm a black man and this doesn't just go for police but it also has other injustices with prosecutors, lawyers, judges, etc. deep down in their inner being. They look at some black people and would not mind seeing them as some kind of slaves again and when they see how some have prospered they get upset and can't deal with it in a way because they are now a part of a stage that is of an unseen suggestion that they have in their life where the pain of who they are and who they want to be take over them and a slave-owner mentality that kicks in and they think of blacks as not being equal and they want to keep them down. You can call this a blindness and sickness that affects the judgment call they make. What is a part of the black hole in someone's soul that works with the void-noid sin-drome?

Now to unveil the darkness of some people is not my call but the wisdom of the Lord in the right time in history therefore look to the heavens and given thanks that freedom comes to all who may possess this past tense of darkness we pray for them.

Today could this be the discovery of a new sickness? Not by a long shot. It is an old presence of the prince of darkness who has only one kind of presence to fulfill and that is the prejudice it carries for all who can have a love for the Lord. That is why Satan can shape his trickery and present it, mold it, divide it, pretty it up if he wants to, just to make it look good, feel good or anything else to give it an appeal so you will be attracted to it and make you think it is right and what is that, sin, the factor that has unseen strings attached to it they want you to believe there is nothing wrong with it.

Now does the fact of this trouble you? If so, good, therefore you can see change needs to take place. I also have to reveal the sickness of some black people noting b bola-bola. Does this unwanted place of mind that carries a sickness have time to stop harming its people to end its reign of terror? I think so and that ends in 2012 but the after affect will not stop it all because the message will not be received by all. So the residue will still come to pass in the ways of darkness that harm people. That is why the people need to take a hold to their own added protection from the Lord.

Therefore would some of the people in the world be better off not seeing not hearing and not talking than to have all of these things added to their life if it will deny them life at the end of this earthly one.

Does the Lord have revealed something only when mankind can have a need to accept them only? I think so. Do we as a people accept this wisdom and will the jury come back with the right verdict?

Could this new way of living put a twist on the judgment of the police problem? Therefore, in the past and the future we shouldn't have time to fight a fight that the Lord needs to fight so we can win. So if you are not aware of this and who you are and what you are doing and call yourself grown, don't fool yourself even if I and others are fooled by you.

To The Innocent

We can believe that someone can lead lots of others in the right ways to lead. Therefore finish this book to help fix things you don't understand!

I have learned that some people want to tame the savage beast in others so badly they go out of their way trying to beat it out of them. What happens is the spark of the Lord in them brings them to a point that they don't know how to handle it and before they can get a grip on themselves, they act like they are judge and jury and executioner and it overwhelms them and that is not of the Lord. Satan makes them think they are greater than they are in doing this which puts them on the wrong side of the law and the Lord.

Now, do others have this same problem? Yes, all people in the world have it even good people sometimes make this mistake also bad people. It is a part of Satan's trickery. Therefore, don't fall into a trap that will give you a rap sheet by knowing the good from the bad in you to stay in a good state of mind.

Hypothetical Perplex; I Think Not

Now does being unwise make you foolish? You better believe it does. So if you had a choice, would you keep on the blinders as if you were in the race of life as a horse where when running sometimes around the track to just win or take them off?

Some would like to know if it is a spark of the Lord in you, why would it let you betray yourself? It is the power that it possesses that can't be controlled by mankind. When mankind tries to it can destroy itself at the same time.

It is not a toy or joke. It is one of humans' most prized possession and if it is used as the Lord wants it to be, it can do the greatest of things or if it is tried to be used for one's self in a selfish way that it should not be it will bring death to someone in their life sooner than it should be or at the end of their life. The gift of the spirit of the Lord in every human being is to not be compromised by us. It is to be manifested only with the praise and worship with the Lord by giving thanks to allow his control over it in you only.

Then the more you know the more you grow in his name within you because it is his power he trusts in you to be used in his will and not in yours. That is why so many have the ungodliness in their struggles to try to fight for self-righteousness and it is not their righteousness because they forgot they have done nothing for their grace and mercy but they act like it is owed to them and that is so untrue.

Could this be the straw that broke the camel's back? The fact that if a law enforcement officer was told to do one thing and they did something else before they knew it, that a man being taken down and then was told to use a taser on the man and they grabbed their gun and shot and killed the man and apologized and said it was an accident give notice that some white officers have a thing called Anglo-bola against black people whether conscious or subconscious that can be fixed with the wisdom of love that is within this message from the Lord. Don't get caught up in the A+B Bola-bola or the B+A Bola-bola in a sense of a perspective of a fight against one another, people can fix self.

Therefore, it is nice to now be able to get off the train ride that the void-noid sin-drome try to get some people to stay on until they make a mistake they can't take back because it may start off as a smooth ride but if you don't get off, it will crash. How do you get off? Jump into the arms of the Lord now to keep you safe now jump to avoid the lumps.

The pain of others that have to face this darkness on both sides is not a pain that has escaped me. Now I can start to rest my pain that, as a messenger of peace, has been put in place for all others to share in the stopping of this war of an ungodly kind in order to meet in the valley with love. From my tears and others' tears that have made a pond where still waters run, put to rest and drown this problem in the past of our history.

Time to Lose

It is time to lose the retardedness in one's self. It is worse than the mentally challenged problems in or on a moral sense that come in a state of mind that is not wise. The message that I have learned about is not a present I want my people to possess and that is the Caucasian persuasion will not stop killing black men until they meet the black opposition in the same way that they have been after all of these hundreds of years. I beg to differ because in order to make ourselves better we must see that your problem is our problem and if we learn of a solution then it is up to us to believe in you to make it right. Therefore the burden that the trickery of Satan that was put on you, you no longer have. It is now another part of mankind's past that has been put in place to replace hate with love. Even if it is the deep down part of it you may not know you have had. Don't let this be a roadblock; it has been removed.

Know This

This is a weapon of mass compassion – the brothers of a nation of people want to march against the police. They feel after the hundreds of years they want to pick up arms against them. So the Lord gave me the instruction to put this together and prevent a calamity of the two that will not make the right present of the life we need to love. We can stop the violence with the new level of treatment with wisdom.

Therefore we the people forgive you for the places you really didn't want to go. I like to think I can take my writing to a new hemisphere that bypasses this atmosphere; with the enlightening of the youth in Christ to keep them out of a war to keep their freedom to help also empty a part of the jail system more and more.

We All

We all can learn to grow up in the ways of non-violence. We don't want this to be a part of the straw that broke the camel's back but to be looked at as the needle we found in the haystack; the avenue that I had (and now we have) uncover to cover up in life.

We don't want the trials of a kind of tribulation in the death of anyone at our new space in history. Therefore, don't confuse the two, spirituality and practicality because they are not the same, but common sense always comes in handy.

Iconic Not Ironic

Is it evident that this is a problem that Black Americans and other ethnicities don't have by them not adding the additional harm to another nation of whites or minorities as a police officer? If so, it is not the norm on a basis that others do it's only some of the Caucasian officers who have this kind of problem or ailment. That may or may not be their fault believe it or not. The writing is on the chart even if it sounds off the wall.

Isaiah 54:4

4. Do not be afraid: you will not suffer shame. Do not fear disgrace; you will not be humiliated. You will forget the shame of your youth and remember no more the reproach of your widowhood.

Not yourself because of your past down with shame up with fame.

If the black cops were killing the white young men like they did we would help to put a stop to it.

Truly Now

Believe you are not alone in the battle of self-growth outside of self with others as a true peace officer. But knowing that sometimes to not be able to see clearly in a battlefield that has no line of sight can be done with the eyes of the Lord lighting your way.

About the Author
I Am Thankful

I was born in the back woods of Mississippi in my grandparents' home with the assistance of a midwife who was paid a quart of buttermilk and a pound of cheese and a lot of love from my family.

I also believe that what I write was planted by the Lord in me that told me one day to bring forth the working of the words I would write to help write some of the wrong in mankind. Therefore it gives me great pride to announce the breaking of a curse that was aimed at black people to harm them by way of the use of the laws that mankind had put in place, to get away with murder at one time in the history of America.

It is now written so the ancestors that have prayed for a change to come that have seen their love once harmed and killed can rest a little more at peace that the shutting down of a part of the ungodly system mankind had let be put in place has ended on this level of harm to the non-white people who have been harmed by it.

Prayers for this issue can now be moved to another problem. By way of the answers we have received we can help stop the lack of love. I thank you for your prayers; without them over the last 400 years things may not have reached this level of freedom and change with the revealing and understanding of this wisdom.

Knowing no one should have to participate in anyone's spiritual war that has hit the ground level of wanting someone else in it other than the Lord is not wise because no one else can help and sometimes people want to pull others into a spiritual war they are having to help and others get hurt because we as humans sometimes take good for bad and bad for good and if we don't know our Lord as well as we need to or should. He will leave us to our own devices to try to correct a problem until we can't then if we don't seek the Lord's counseling and wisdom we are on our own.

Therefore the spiritual battle has only one who has been in it and it was the first one in heaven when the high angel and crew tried to take over heaven and challenge the Lord God.

That is why we trust his son Jesus to send help by way of the angels to help with spiritual warfare that he has the know-how and experience to win. Additionally, it is not good to fight when someone may not be your enemy and you look just to win in some or any way because you are going to lose when fighting a spiritual war with Satan along with the fact that it is ironic that almost all people that are in a fight with Satan in a spiritual war and someone doesn't know they are in one until it may be too late. They have done the wrong thing to try to fix something in the way they think it should be corrected but the sad part is when two people are in their own spiritual war and try to take it out on each other because that is what people do subconsciously or use others to make them feel good: how sick can some people become? God knows.

I give this personal note I have been there in a spiritual war with a close family member and if I didn't know who was in charge, I may not be here to write this and it was sickening just the same.

I believe the wars that are going on in the so-called third world or eastern countries are mostly because of the spiritual wars that Satan has tricked them into in a state of being in one way or another to fight for an unworthy cause or the power of greed and the business of a people and none of this makes sense because we did not have war in the beginning of mankind, but we do now because of what the angels who became Satan's followers brought with him to earth and it is of a spirit of death. It can only draw death to it.

What is it people want you to fight with the devil that got up in them from its spiritual presence and that is the top and bottom of it. Now don't think because some of you are churchgoers to the house of God, it makes you right because some people take Satan or a demon to the church with them to get it out. So before you think you are praising the Lord, first try to pray to receive his wisdom.

Sin Death

One of the worse things in the world someone could have is a fear of self and it makes them kill someone else. This is one thing that Satan drives people to the level of. It is not really the fear of others but their own death. Foremost, it is backwards thinking place that some people need to come out of for their own good because people really kill themselves with or from not knowing the Lord in the right way.

Situations

We all may end up in difficult situations but it does not define who we are. What are the things that are important to the Lord? Love Him and your neighbor. Righteousness in the Lord is to be right with him.

This is a wake-up call for the law enforcement officers introducing who calls themselves officers of the law. Jail time and God's hell time will be made available to you if you don't get correct. Take the protection; he is waiting to provide it.

Experience This

Because the people with the most experience are needed.

If this scripture reminds you of you it is a sign of the necessary changes that are possible to achieve. Look to your help for your inadequacies.

Psalms 46:1-3, 10-11
1. God is our refuge and strength, an ever-present help in trouble.

2. therefore we will not fear, though the earth give way and the mountains fall into the heart of the sea,
3. though its waters roar and foam and the mountains quake with their urging.

10. Be still, and know that I am God; I will be exalted among the nations, I will be exalted in the earth.
11. The Lord Almighty is with us; the God of Jacob is our fortress.

Seek and You Shall Find
Getting With It

Getting back to one of the main points of it all - As a nation, we are weakening our defense and must move forward to not be caught off guard. We can and must show the world that we are all for one and one for all and all in to obtain our own self-respect.

We are all a part of the problem if we are not doing our part to solve it. Therefore get with a program you may need to be with in order for spiritual growth to occur in your life. if we all do this everything will come together right now.

A Great Thought to Have

Who am I in my writing? I am you to a certain degree.

Know This

The Lord gives us the power to avoid the void-noid sin-drome to not be brought down and out of life by Satan.

This Wisdom

This wisdom is a present and is presented to the uncommon things within mankind because it is not common of mankind to use this kind of strength in their daily lives. It is not of their truth and it is of a truth that some people don't want to know about that happens in their lives. Therefore to help stop all of the not righteous thoughts that may run across your mind from time to time.

Tell yourself I am aware of the void-noid sin-drome I denounce it; I don't take dictation from it, I don't play with it; I don't see it as a part of my life now and forever thanks to my Lord.

Now give someone a book to help them to stop feeding the crook in themselves. The mission is to stop the "would be", unknown crook that is within some people.

This battle has already been won when we understand how to let the Lord step in to fight for use also be thankful there could have been more lost youth to a problem some officer may have.

This book may be far from the most well written book you have ever read but the point it makes is clear as daylight.

Let Something Out

Now what can make this clearer? The one thing that comes to mind is there are almost or none of the issues that black officers have with killing white civilians who are under arrest. That may be because of them being in the void-noid sin-drome. Therefore it is a separation of a problem that somewhat affects the white people only. Now it is obvious that some people get problems that come by way of their ethnicity as the black on black crimes issue that they have. But there is a way out for all to help solve their problems.

All people can avoid the void-noid sin-drome by knowing the wisdom to be used that comes from the Lord.

The End Justifies the Means

This is a justice that we should serve under that we had not been using to end problems.

How Now

We can't expect the Lord to do something that we can do for ourselves; can we? We can't because he gives us things to do for him to help.

A Fact; Not Fiction

The ways of the Lord lies within I know about more of it now.

Blessed

It is not blessed if you will and blessed if you won't, it is blessed if it is his will and not blessed if you don't.

This isn't any kind of zinger it is a hands on principle of prestige of the heavenly kind.

Time to Have

It is time to have a fun spirit to come along with you and all that you do with your time.

We pray for a new beginning

I wish for us to lose the pain of the kind of dilemma that currently plagues our lives so that our lifetimes show the better side of life. What a new way to put a book to bed in order to create rest that we have had to look forward to that is now here.

Please let the people who have passed on now rest in peace with the time we have left together on earth.

There are some issues you won't find a way out of by yourself; so get help.

Welcome to the Slaying of One of the Last Void-Noid Dragons That May be Hiding Inside of You

This is the invisible dragon slayer shield to be shared by all. We believe it is a timely and necessary message. We did not feel the need for professional editing.

In Another Land

They are having what they call Holy wars in other lands that lots of people believe in but it really is a spiritual war with a lot of people involved. Now if they learn to end the war with themselves. They somewhat can end one fight and get two wins.

I May Take a Bit of a "Lipping" for This

To keep it real, I have found through my personal interactions with police officers that a combative nature that some black men (young and adult) take toward white officers enhances the creation of a negative response from the white officers. This is a description that has to be amended in the African American population. It has also been evidenced in the Latina and other minority ethnicities in America. This amendment must take place as an individual creed of positive change.

We as a people came here from a void-noid space that we learn how to fill in to become whole as we are meant to be without help we can stay there. It started off from a baby but even if we are grown, it sometimes still needs some blanks filled in to end some poverty. That is what this book can help do to avoid the blackness of the traps Satan has set up for people that comes from many directions and these are a few traps the Lord has sprung to not have his people to step in to end a part of the madness and sadness.

If any of this writing offends anyone, I did my best with the staff I had in the editing of this material.

Do not only call this writing interesting, try to make it transitional for your comfort, convenience and benefit.

"Extendation" – a new way of making things last. A good and positive relationship between the police and the people will hopefully be achieved through this "Extendation".

There are relationships that I know of where the higher officers of the law used the judgment of the Lord that I know of to free a black man who was innocent in the eyes of the Lord and mankind in the old justice system would somewhat massacre him with time and the system never got it and at the same time kept him free without strings attached to them. That was when God's law stood taller than all others.

As one of the police officials said, "It has been over 40 years since they have had this kind of a war of mayhem in the City of Baltimore." Is it that it took the 40 years of a development of strife and prejudice to end the poverty of an ugly part of black humanity? If so; now all people can witness. Does that mean a 40 year reign of some kind of terror that took place before it broke the dam before a part of hell broke loose?

If We Didn't Know Any Better; Now We Do

When the war of this kind of injustice came about it had to be. It is no longer needed because the point has been proven. But does Satan want to trick others to think it is needed again? Yes he does; to get people harmed because that is his sport and the game he plays.

New weapons of peace are here to be used and shared to help stop the warfare that has plagued people in the past. The facts are in; one way streets have turned into two way streets. Now, even if the people who sit in high places who work with Satan that try to make war by not doing the right thing, we don't have to fall into the trap that harms us as the prince of darkness thinks we should. He wants our foolishness to outweigh our wisdom, if we didn't know to riot again is not the right thing to do about what happen.

The stopping of so much black on black harm has run its course from 1972 to 2012. That is Phase 1

Now the next harm to the black man from the police officer has ran its course from 1975 to 2015. That is Phase 2

Now the last level of destroying the black males is the injustice system to cut their ties to Satan's chain gang mentality that harms them with a disregard of rehabilitation. It too will end - date forthcoming. That is Phase 3

Why was this a problem in the first place? I can only blame it on one thing. I point my finger and the blame at Satan and the one fact that Satan may have place it upon the black man because he came to help the Lord carry the cross that he was crucified on. What a payback he thought that may last forever that now creates a power of love that he meant for destruction.

As of today, as black people, we are not in a corner about this problem anymore, dated April 27, 2015.

We can stop more of what we do to each other with the book *Why Do Black Men Harm Each Other More Than Others?* (containing information about the cause and the cure). Additionally, youth can learn to stop the blackness that doesn't have a thing to do with the color of one's skin, with in a copy of *The New Added Protection for the Development of Teens and Young Adults At Risk*. This book can help stop the wrong ways that young people go sometimes.

To help end the situations where so many people live on the edge as it relates to the police and the people, I would like to introduce the book titled, *Time to Stop Living on the Edge*. It is a way to come back from a place that can exist in the mindset that you can be pulled back off of with a renewal of spiritual health. Now try this garment on, it can make you feel better and take you away from the edge.

To help you to treat yourself new send for a copy of *A Crown for Kings and Queens* also *What Two Can Easily Do*; or try *To the New Wise Men*. To receive the copy email tb.bthpm@gmail.com.

It was a shame that I cry on my birthday because of the killings at a high school in Chardon, Ohio.

This was a gray area that is now crystal clear.

As the new people of culture from all nations that make up America, we now see ourselves in this new way in this new day.

You Know

When people display a wolf pack mentality in a situation involving child endangerment between other youths; it too crosses all cultures. Please stop it; all that is left to do now is eradicate this problem.

We Can

Stop these personal hate crimes by young or babes in the woods with our new growth as American adults in Christ.

One or a few bad apples don't spoil the whole bunch. Therefore, if we as a people don't rule over ourselves when a foolish thing is done to someone that is an officer of the law, we become a part of the spoiling of the bunch as if we are one of them. Then Satan wins. To not include yourself in the grand level of this kind of spiritual warfare, pray for peace and don't think you are fighting for love and it is darkness that you are fighting for and you should know it.

Now

If you ask if my or your love will grow with this I do think so. Is this a part of our rainbow? I know for me what about you? Come and help me find me create more rainbows together. We can't see precursors to prevent curses. So how can I be a simple kind of man?

Separation

At a time in our lives we will or should separate from something when times come do it with pride. You too can become bombastic in your voice. Then have a steak without something at stake. It is our epic time together.

Know now you don't have any kind of scorpion nature but a biblical nature and don't cast your pearls on the swine.

We don't need to add to mankind's confusion. It has enough to do to make things right. Stop the madness that only can give us more sadness. In the name of the Lord be still and let the Lord show you how to get to his lighthouse. Amen

Now to rebuild the trust we need as people on both sides, first you have to trust yourself with the protection of the Lord against the principalities of not letting darkness falls upon your life. To do this it will keep you free from the bondage of Satan because he incites the riots and the civil unrest of people in all lands on earth. Look to the heavens for the peace we need to share.

Stopping the civil unrest with levels of peace is needed. It is time to stop the sea of bloodshed.

The Show of the Covering

Be ye under the power that allows the wings of an angel to stop you and protect you as if you are a child of God as was shown when the children were about to get on a bus and a vehicle drove in front of them but couldn't harm them because of what the Lord saw coming and put a stop to it to not let pain come into their lives. It is truly a hallelujah moment.

It is time to stop the spiritual craziness in the world with our home land first!

Be Careful Who You Listen To

If you think you are listening to the Spirit be sure that it is the Spirit and not you.

At This Time

Time to stop all the tension that is running through our land with knowing the Lord loves us.

Noah's Way

Today if you are the people who are now a part of the spiritual skills land of love you are now walking in the land of the Noah's way of grace in the Lord on the earthly place that you dwell in. Thank God for the Noah's way to go into live in your life. Noah was a man who was given a plan by the Lord yet he was not perfect but obedient.

In order to never have another incident such as the one happening in Baltimore, MD involving the death of an unarmed citizen under arrest, please spread the news of Noah's way.

Think

If you think we have gotten off the same beaten path of the way this book may have supposed to be going, you are right and the reason is to bring a vision to the way we as people can stop being violent and lighting the fuse the way we have done in the past from not knowing how to actually defuse a violent presence of people.

Therefore, the one thing that all people who understand the things we need to do can say they took away from this book that is also considered priceless is the faith healing of one's self on a better level of life; that is right now. So spread that news that you are a faith healer and have an obligation to help others become one also. I thank you for you are in my heart I announce this knowledge before my Lord and in his name.

Thanks to the people and their efforts on one level or another that we don't need to employ anymore, even though we learned to receive the piece of peace from it to keep forever.

Note

There are no tiny tunes in this song in the keys of sight!

What Niceness

To be able to get your feet wet and not feel like you are going to drown is a civil way to walk out of a march of victory.

Remember we never have to act like a bunch of renegades we are civilized. Also if you still feel a little twisted about coming in to a better you do the twist by yourself or out on the dance floor or in a crowd of people at a rally. Then after the dance get something "kool" to drink.

When we know how to understand these things the gathering doesn't turn into a mob state of darkness or become the robbing mob that burns down businesses and is hell bent on destruction.

Know that you don't have to be a part of the void-noid because you may think you have become non-human in your status of reality it is only the prince of darkness trying to get over on you.

This method of understanding can also help stop a cop from being a bully.

I appreciate the parent/guardian who will step up and step in to make sure their children don't become a part of the "mob" mentality.

Today's Intervention
May 8, 2015

I was feeling somewhat insecure about a friend of mine and gave them a call only to find out that there was trouble in their mindset and spirit. They were unable to explain what the problem was over the phone so I went there immediately. Once I arrived, I saw three bailiffs from the sheriff's department who were ready to subdue my friend because of his unbalanced state of mind. Two were white and one was black. When I asked what was going on, the first thing the black officer said was "thank you for coming. I was praying that someone came to assist us in getting this individual to understand that he will have to leave the premises because he had been evicted.

I then started talking with my friend to let he know that he had to comply or he would find himself in trouble. He and I began to disagree and he calmed down and collected himself enough where a confrontation was avoided. At that time things started to settle down. The black officer and I walked over to a private area and again he told me he was grateful I came because the other two officers who were white did not know how to handle a situation dealing with this black man and his unbalanced mental state of mind.

I know if I had not come by someone would have gotten hurt badly and it would have become another national incident that Satan would have enjoyed. To make a long story short God's intervention prevented an escalation of an unfortunate event. I did present the information about this book to them. They said this may be a great tool for others to have in situations like this. At the end, we all departed in peace.

Now you don't have to have an emotionally unstable life

I personally know someone who was a long-time friend of one of the people who were killed by police officers in Cleveland, Ohio. The friend of his said he had a problem with the fear of guns.

We can make things new and create a game changer. Do the people learn to give a new perspective to each other? Yes, with the scales of justice equaling out more for all. I believe so and so should all begin to think positive.

People I want you to know that if you pick this book apart you should know it may almost take you a lifetime. But, as you can learn to think on a blink when it is a part of God's plan.

In Conclusion

Don't think I have total pleasure in writing this book or that it is untimely because it is timely. I think if this was written ten-twenty years ago (or more), how much farther we may have been but to know that we are all better from our experience in life, that comes from some of the things we don't or didn't want to happen, still gives an amount of freedom. Therefore, to live with this in the now may be best for all.

Do black Americans feel a new sense of equality at this time in history? Yes and this should mean all Americans should also now that the upper crest has been broken through with the people and now we add to the intent of the law is next and it is the hope of the people that this book will help to fix that also.

I send up and out my prayers for the latest families of the two peace officers of law who were killed in my birth state of Mississippi. It is a tragedy that the person who got caught in the void-noid sin-drome and could not understand the love of his fellow man and the love within themselves. It is my hope that we can put a stop to as much of this senseless killing in the world that we can.

Confronting your own injuries and pain is one of the things Satan doesn't want you to do. The more you do that the less the darkness can hurt you. If Satan keeps you in the blind about yourself the more he can persuade you that there isn't a black hole that you can fall into. Therefore be aware of your shortcomings and work on improving them. The answer tells you to not put on the wrong hat and to keep it halo.

In the opening of a somewhat new discovery of a sickness that has no smell, no obvious sign of a visible trace other than the destruction that it leaves behind. We must take it as serious as a cancer that can be eliminated in our lifetime as a part of the bola-bola have been stopped in its tracks or is being stopped in its tracks.

Together we stand we are not divided any longer as Satan wishes for us to fall. We now have a waterfall of cleansing to stand under.

He Sees Himself in You

What kind of selfie does the Lord take of you?

You Are Worthy

We can remove our shield of shame that keeps the Lord out of our lives more from us not thinking we are worthy of his love and that is so true.

Added Request

This is one of the messages and only God knows how many more messages the Lord may use Bro. Bush to bring forth.

It is so nice to not be able to let go of something that is so good for you: you can't, you won't; you don't.

It is not about what I write it is about the word of the Lord that makes this right as well as real.

The Lord has something for everyone and he has had it broken down to a laymen terminology in books to help people stop being crooks to themselves. In other words, don't be unaware when *you* come to steal, kill and destroy yourself like a thief in the night or day.

It is Not

It is not my will that all of these things come to pass but by the will of the father in heaven and his love for you to restore your soul and make you whole again as he has promised you in his word.

It is time to take off that invisible cocoon of a layer of sin to unveil the righteousness of self.

A great thing to learn is to know how to walk away from a battle you don't belong in.

If you think of Noah's way and how he got drunk and naked be ye at home and have the Lord's garments on one's self, the love of family; then know of it as a mistake and not a habit to forget about it as the Lord will forget also; the past is the past.

Advice

For anyone who doesn't know how to listen to themselves while they are reading; put a cork in your mouth and lightly bite down on it, this will help.

Today is this a part of divine intervention of the Lord? Only you can say this for yourself.

Freedom For the Captive

Jeremiah 29:11
11. For I know the thoughts that I think toward you saith the Lord. Thoughts of peace and not of evil to give you an expected end.
12. Then shall ye call upon me and ye shall go and pray unto me and I will hearken unto you.
13. And ye shall see me and find me when ye shall search for me with all your heart.
14. And I will be found of you saith the Lord. And I will turn away your captivity and I will gather you from all the natures and from all the places whither I have driven you saith the Lord. And I will bring you again unto the place whence I caused to be carried away captive.

It is time to fill the void so you don't become some kind of noid. We can learn to realize on the power of the Lord that he entrusts in us to keep Satan's sin nature behind us.

The intellectual properties are granted to those who are a part of the body and bride of Christ. This is why I say hallelujah for that.

Note: any kind of bola isn't civilized. The problem with the motorcycle gang could have been solved better than the way it went down. The anglo-bola wolf pack mentality brewed and burst and then hit the fan. Now stop it so you can know this new level of love.

Ain't No Sneaking Me by Satan

Dear Lord, thank you for my deliverance from the void-noid sin-drome. I know it came from the loneliness of my spirit not being comforted by your wisdom and now that it is filling up I can see with a new sign that my eyes don't supply the love you have for me that ends the opportunities for the lonely spirit sin-drome to harm me. I thank you with my saying hallelujah to you and can and will testify to this to the world. Now Satan can't sike me out of life because of my spirit being under nourished.

Now there is no more loneliness from the spirit in me from not being nourished, fed and fortified. Henceforth you are in control and not that unknown part of you that can no longer affect you and what you do, as was when you were blinded by the void in your life.

Therefore Satan can't own any of your spiritual property any longer if he has and this agreement has the seal of the eternal blessing on it, stamped by Father God, In Jesus' name.

This is a part of the truth that quenches the fires that can't be seen or heard that you can put out. Now I can thank you if you have accepted this kind of breakfast, lunch and dinner to assure the peace within that comes out of you. Now pick up the word of God and get whatever else it has to offer you. Then you will get a chance to sit in the grandstand and direct the traffic away from Satanville, the city of darkness that most people who wind up there had no idea they were on that road. It may now seem as if it has a road to Damascus you have to follow and the bridge got washed out but we the body of Christ put it back in place.

To help us along the last part of this writing came from the upcoming book that will enhance the opportunity for people to develop spiritual skills. Hopefully you will get a copy so you can see for yourself what a kiss from heaven is like when the Lord puts two of the things he loves together.

Positive Change Is Needed to Create Healing

This is An Article of Faith

(Faith without works is useless; so put your faith to work!)

Note: we are all patriots in this country so let get it together

Once you get this breath of fresh air, we can stop the presence of the way law enforcement conducted services before by trying something new with your spirit and heart into it that can be lived by.

To Help Police

At Bound to Heaven Publishing/Ministries, we have put in place books that allow you to use your common sense (and imagination) to be able to choose the material that you feel you need. It is our hope that you will give thought to your solution of what it is that may take your life out of what could be a dark spot in order for you to find the grace and mercy you are so deserving.

We can only say that we delight in knowing what we have maybe what you need and if you have any questions about your needs, you may contact us to ask us if there is any help that we may be able to provide for you because we will help you make a tailor made choice of information to give you the best result for your effort to solve the issue that maybe making your life uncomfortable.

This is a non-conventional self-help, help-self program
for spiritual advancement and growth

The breaking of bread with love
between two parties with a new kind of love!

Time In

By the time you get to the last pages of this book, I would like to feel how much light you have that has lightened up the dark by way of the Lord's presence in us.

This is a way to become a spiritual warrior who is motivated by love, compassion and the true pursuit of happiness for all people.

The more we control sin the more we eliminate prejudices; believe it and if you don't, try it !

The wisdom within gives a better understanding of why some of the thing happen that may have left some people confused and in disbelief about what happened and even what they may have done.

Time to help the control all Adrenalin rushes
which result in hurt, harm and/or danger!

This is a level of a new spiritual architecture

To Know This is to Grow

Now if you ever feel like you want to get into a spiritual war, make sure you have a heavenly leader to follow.

Psalm 119:105
105. "Thy word is a lamp unto my feet and a light unto my path."

Thank God

We can match all of the ailments with a solution that fits. Thus, knowing spirituality over that which is carnal is the way to make life better.

Endorsements

This book has been endorsed by various individuals, who give it their approval and agree that it is a healthy way by which to think and live, as well as a peaceful resolution to an issue that police and people may be confronted with.

Acts 20:24
24. However, I consider my life worth nothing to me, if only I may finish the race and complete the task the Lord Jesus

has given me-the task of testifying to the gospel of God's grace.

Philippians 4:17
17. Not that I am looking for a gift, but I am looking for what may be credited to your account.

Certificate of Completion

If you completed this book, this can be a certificate of completion to certify that you are no longer thinking on or in a pathway of ungodly principle of life, no matter whether you are in law enforcement or not. Sign it and display it with pride as evidence.

This certificate is issued to you by Bound to Heaven Publishing/Ministries

With Love,
Bro. Tracy E. Bush, Owner and CEO
Bound to Heaven Publishing/Ministries

This book can help bring healing to all people!

Contact Us

For More Information or questions, email us at tb.bthpm@gmail.com

www.ingramcontent.com/pod-product-compliance
Lightning Source LLC
Chambersburg PA
CBHW070522210526
45169CB00027B/276